PENGUIN CLASSICS

ELECTRA AND OTHER PLAYS

ADVISORY EDITOR: BETTY RADICE

SOPHOCLES was born at Colonus, just outside Athens, in 496 B.C., and lived ninety years. His long life spanned the rise and decline of the Athenian Empire; he was a friend of Pericles, and though not an active politician he held several public offices, both military and civil. The leader of a literary circle and friend of Herodotus, he was interested in poetic theory as well as practice, and he wrote a prose treatise *On the Chorus*. He seems to have been content to spend all his life at Athens, and is said to have refused several invitations to royal courts.

Sophocles first won a prize for tragic drama in 468, defeating the veteran Aeschylus. He wrote over a hundred plays for the Athenian theatre, and is said to have come first in twenty-four contests. Only seven of his tragedies are now extant, these being *Ajax*, *Antigone*, *Oedipus the King*, *Women of Trachis*, *Electra*, *Philoctetes*, and the posthumous *Oedipus at Colonus*. A substantial part of *The Searches*, a satyr play, was recovered from papyri in Egypt in modern times. Fragments of other plays remain, showing that he drew on a wide range of themes; he also introduced the innovation of a third actor in his tragedies. He died in 406 B.C.

E. F. WATLING was educated at Christ's Hospital and University College, Oxford. His translations of Greek and Roman plays for the Penguin Classics include the seven plays of Sophocles, nine plays of Plautus, and a selection of the tragedies of Seneca. He died in 1990.

SOPHOCLES

ELECTRA AND OTHER PLAYS

★

AJAX / ELECTRA

WOMEN OF TRACHIS

PHILOCTETES

★

TRANSLATED BY E. F. WATLING

PENGUIN BOOKS

PENGUIN BOOKS

Published by the Penguin Group
Penguin Books Ltd, 27 Wrights Lane, London W8 5TZ, England
Penguin Books USA Inc., 375 Hudson Street, New York, New York 10014, USA
Penguin Books Australia Ltd, Ringwood, Victoria, Australia
Penguin Books Canada Ltd, 10 Alcorn Avenue, Toronto, Ontario, Canada M4V 3B2
Penguin Books (NZ) Ltd, 182–190 Wairau Road, Auckland 10, New Zealand

Penguin Books Ltd, Registered Offices: Harmondsworth, Middlesex, England

This translation first published 1953
25 27 29 30 28 26

Printed in England by Clays Ltd, St Ives plc
Set in Monotype Bembo

*The terms for the performance of these plays may
be obtained from the Society of Authors,
84 Drayton Gardens, London SW10 9SD,
to whom all applications for
permission should be
made*

CONTENTS

*

INTRODUCTION

In his long life of ninety years (496-406 B.C.) Sophocles wrote over a hundred plays for the Athenian theatre. Of these only seven are extant, ranging in date from about his fiftieth year to the date of his death. As his earliest known victory, in the competitive dramatic festivals in which such plays were produced, was in the year 468 B.C., it may be presumed that the surviving plays form a representative sample of his best work and that that work was mainly the product of his middle and later life. It would be interesting if we could point with certainty to any example of his earliest essays in tragedy, or know at what age he first made any mark in the theatre. Only in the case of Aristophanes do we know that a man in his early twenties could obtain a hearing on the comic stage; the masters of tragedy seem to have served a longer apprenticeship.*

The plays translated in this volume (and placed in their probable chronological order) show some differences of style and treatment, but it is difficult – partly owing to the uncertainty of date in some cases – to trace any progressive development in one direction or another.

Its general shape and style place *Ajax* among the earlier works, and its position, in the oldest collections, at the head of the list, indicates a strong tradition of its having been the earliest of the extant plays. A preponderance of long speeches and soliloquies, and the comparatively rare appearance of more than two speakers together (other than the Chorus) are consistent with the early style of tragedy as established by Aeschylus. Even so, the play does not lack characteristically Sophoclean features. Its opening scene is as realistic in tone and dramatic in movement as that of any of his later plays; and the

*For a fuller account of Sophocles' place in the Greek theatre and his relation to Aeschylus and Euripides, see the Introduction to *The Theban Plays* in this series.

treatment of the Chorus, strongly characterized and closely concerned in the action of the play, is much more 'advanced' than, for instance, that of *Women of Trachis* and is very similar to that of *Philoctetes,* a work of much later date. If *Ajax* is in fact our earliest example of Sophoclean tragedy, it already shows strong indications of the new life which our author was to bring into the Athenian theatre.

One feature of the construction of the play may not be easily understood at first sight, but is of importance in relation to its central theme. Rising to a climax at the death of Ajax, the play seems to 'peter out' in a protracted and undignified squabble over the disposal of his remains. The fact is that the *death* of Ajax is not the true climax nor the central interest of the play. Greek tragedy does not as a rule take the Shakespearean shape of 'The Life and Death of —'; in this case it starts with the death, or at any rate the downfall, of its hero, and its ultimate concern is with the judgement we are to make, through the minds of his friends or enemies, of the hero's character. So that though admittedly (and, we must suppose, intentionally) the language of the play drops to a more prosaic level in the closing scenes, the keen debate over the burial of Ajax must have been to the Greek audience the most significant part of the play. I fancy that its effect may have been somewhat similar to that of the debate of the Knights, in *Murder in the Cathedral,* over the death of the Archbishop. In addition, of course, the religious importance of burial (as we see in *Antigone*) was a vital factor in the situation.

Typical of the Greek conception of tragedy is the theme of the great man fallen, the strange enigma of weakness and strength combined in one being. This problem Sophocles was to explore again, in Oedipus and in Heracles and doubtless other instances now lost to us; in *Ajax* he has presented it in a comparatively simple but highly concentrated form.

In *Electra* Sophocles handles one stage of the great story

which Aeschylus had told in the three parts of his Orestean trilogy. As Euripides also used the theme in his *Electra* (whether before or after Sophocles is not known for certain) the approach of the three tragedians to the same subject can here be closely compared. Except for some minor details the basic story is the same, but differences in the treatment arise from the method and artistic aims of the three writers. For Aeschylus the story is only significant in its full development from the first sin of the ancestor to the final release of Orestes from the load of guilt; and in presenting the saga in the form of three consecutive plays his concern is primarily with the power and continuity of the divine forces which control the destinies of the doomed family – forces which cannot be questioned or resisted. The persons of the drama are less individuals than puppets symbolic of men and women entrapped in the predicaments to which humanity is condemned. Man is involved in such and such conflicts by the will of heaven, and only heaven can pronounce the verdict and unravel the knot.

Euripides took one chapter of the story – the return of Orestes and the punishment of the murderers – and presented it, in the main, on a human and naturalistic level, yet expressing in his way a judgement on the problem of the story – the judgement, in fact, of a rebel against the accepted interpretation: the deed of Orestes, by Euripides' account, was both inevitable and sinful, and cannot have been the will of any good power. Orestes kills his mother, bitterly protesting against the horror of the deed to which he is driven, and the epilogue of the play foreshadows the torment which his soul is doomed to suffer, imprisoned in a maze of evil from which there is no escape.

Sophocles pronounces no judgement. He neither approves nor condemns. Here, he says to us, is the story – an immortal story, but a story of mortal beings; such was their predicament; such were the pleas advanced on this side and on that; such was the bearing of the persons implicated in the event.

And within the limits assigned to the play, what is done is complete and final. If there was a sequel, we are not concerned with it, except in so far as we supply one for ourselves in our reflexions after the fall of the curtain. More objective than either Aeschylus or Euripides, Sophocles imitates neither the symbolism and poetic sublimity of the elder writer nor the fierce partisanship of the younger. Yet we cannot think that he ignored or belittled the controversial implications of the legend. Rather his feeling seems to have been that it was enough to show the picture, without writing a moral underneath it.

Women of Trachis, the only one of the seven known plays to bear a title denoting the persons of the Chorus, is, oddly enough, the one in which the Chorus is least important; the 'Trachinian women' make no contribution to the plot, their presence at the scene of action has little probability, and their lyric interludes are uninspired. Should the play have been called *Deianeira,* or *Heracles?* That it was not so labelled may be a hint that the author himself was in two minds as to the real subject of the play. It is on this score, at any rate, that its construction has been criticized. If its theme is the love and tragic error of Deianeira, her abrupt death comes too soon, to be followed by an irrelevant postscript in the protracted agony of Heracles. If Heracles is the subject, his appearance is too long delayed and Deianeira's part over-written.

One answer to such criticism is the view that the sense of Deianeira's presence remains with us throughout the closing stages of the tragedy, both in the consequences of her action and in the words spoken of her by Hyllus and Heracles. But since her husband's only thought of her at this point is one of revenge and baffled rage, and no resolution of the conflict is achieved, this view of the matter hardly helps to justify and define the structure of the play. The centre and focus of its theme is surely Heracles – Heracles as seen through the eyes of his wife. In Deianeira Sophocles has drawn one of his most complete and convincing characters, and yet all we know of her is her single-minded devotion to her husband. Through three-quarters of the play Heracles, though absent in person, is kept continually present to our minds – the very fact of his absence being indeed the mainspring of the action – so that his eventual appearance, prepared for by the 'build-up' of the preceding scenes (perhaps the most remarkable example of 'build-up' in all dramatic literature!), far from being an anti-climax, is the true climax of the play. That the husband and wife never meet, but speak of each other across a gulf of terrible misunderstanding, and die apart, gives a last twist of pathos, and a grim dramatic justice, to the conjugal tragedy.

The character given to Heracles in this play does not, by any human standards, endear him to the modern reader. How the ancient audience would feel about the moral problem of the play, it is hard to say. Is Sophocles thinking in terms of human life and contemporary morality? Partly, but not, by the nature and limitations of the story, wholly. Heracles had a clearly defined place in mythology as the symbol of masculine physical strength committed to endless warfare against the powers of evil. That was the justification, and the burden, of his existence, overriding all other loyalties or moral obligations. And if the physical burden was his, on his wife fell the burden of anxiety, loneliness, and neglect. Deianeira knows this. 'Any woman', she says, 'who has known this, will know what kind of thing I suffer.' If Heracles is too much of a superman to interest us as a man, Deianeira is never more than a woman, in her much-tried patience, her bravely subdued pride, and her desperate bid for victory. Heracles moves in a far-off world of monsters and miracles, but Deianeira lives in any street in Athens. With all its defects, some of them due to the intractability of the material which Sophocles chose for the experiment, the play is worthy of its place in the canon, if only as an example of his 'Euripidean' manner, and of the human verisimilitude which he could impart to an unprepossessing, almost repulsive, piece of mythology.

Among the plays nominally classed as tragedies in the Greek theatre, a few (such as the *Iphigeneia in Tauris* of Euripides) break out of the usual pattern of conflict mounting to a climax in violent action. The conflict and the passion (in the sense of suffering) are in the background or antecedents of the story and the play depicts an aftermath issuing in escape or release from tension. Of such a kind is *Philoctetes*.

This play, produced in 409 B.C. (the author's eighty-seventh year) is remarkable both for its atmosphere and for its plot, and shows us our author still experimenting in the theatre and still finding new ways of broadening and varying its interest. The scene of the play is of a new kind, a lonely island in the Aegean, and great skill has gone to the creation, in dialogue, narration, and lyrics, of an appropriate and convincing setting. In what literal sense Sophocles was 'the inventor of scene-painting' we cannot now be sure; but in this play at least it is clear that he did not need to rely on paint and canvas to take the place of verbal scene-painting. The sound of the sea and the birds, the scud of winds and rain, the heat and cold, summers and winters, are with us on every page of the play.

The plot presents a new kind of conflict and a new kind of *dénouement*. There is no violent death, no vengeance or retribution. The tragedies, individual and general, of the Trojan War, are in the background of the story and are kept continually in mind, but the foreground is occupied by a conflict which can be formalized as: physical weakness plus moral strength *versus* physical superiority plus moral weakness. Philoctetes is physically at the mercy of his opponents, Neoptolemus and Odysseus, who could easily force their will upon him, and almost do so; but, as Neoptolemus well knows, might is not right, and without right (here symbolized by the bow in the hands of its rightful owner) might cannot prosper. The

conflict is not in itself exceptional – we are reminded of the
situation between Creon and Antigone – but in the present
play a new dramatic interest is developed in the situation and
character of Neoptolemus, for it is he who finds himself placed
on both sides of the battle, first as the accomplice, not alto-
gether unwilling, of the unscrupulous Odysseus, and then,
true to his better nature, standing out for justice. He has his reward in a solution, under the guidance of Heracles, which both
satisfies his conscience and achieves the object of his mission.
The sympathetic and sensitive picture of Neoptolemus gives
the play an unusual charm and is one of Sophocles' highest
achievements in character-drawing.

The significance of Sophoclean drama, in relation to the religious and ethical climate of his time, has been explored in
books of greater scope and authority than this.   In my series
of translations, with the briefest of incidental comment, I have
tried to set before the English play-reader an impression of the
work of the dramatist who, if he did not actually lay its foun-
dations, was the first to give to theatrical art in ancient Greece
a shape and structure recognizably akin to its modern descen-
dant. And it is to his achievement as a dramatic artist that I
should like finally to direct the reader's attention.

Sophocles was a master of dramatic technique – its inventor,
to all intents and purposes. And it is to one seemingly small
and, like many other momentous discoveries, simple innovation that we owe the astonishing leap which he made from a
comparatively primitive and restricted art-form to the complete 'roundness' of dramatic presentation. The elder master,
Aeschylus, had shown what could be done with *poetry spoken
in character*, and had made the first step from declamatory or
narrative monologue to the exhibition of dramatic conflict in
dialogue between two characters. The step was an important
one, yet did not constitute an essentially significant advance

from the territory of epic poetry, where speech can follow speech in debate or conflict of wills. Sophocles, as Aristotle laconically informs us, 'increased the number of actors to three'.

The mere mechanical advantage of this innovation was a considerable gain; with the triangular scene it became possible to depict a new variety of dramatic situations: a transaction between two persons being hastened, obstructed, or deflected, by the intervention of a third (Orestes, Aegisthus, Electra; Philoctetes, Neoptolemus, Odysseus) – information brought by one person evoking different reactions in each of two others (Clytaemnestra, Electra, Tutor; Oedipus, Messenger, Jocasta) – an attempted deception unmasked (Deianeira, Lichas, Messenger). Aeschylus, in his latest plays, made occasional use of the third actor; but it must be remembered that Sophocles won his first success in the theatre ten years before the production of the *Oresteia* of Aeschylus. So that there is, on the face of it, no reason to doubt the truth of Aristotle's dictum. Sophocles invented the three-actor scene.

But the matter goes deeper than a mere improvement in scene-construction. The essence of the three-actor scene is that the turn of events will depend on whether A will side with B or with C; whether the combined efforts of B and C will change A's purpose; and so on. A choice is to be made, and the choice will be determined by the nature, as well as the situation, of the person making it; character, not predestined event, is now the focus of the drama. Thus, in the hands of Sophocles, drama became not only triangular but three-dimensional; to the length and breadth of mythical narrative he added the depth of human character as he observed it in his fellow mortals. What had hitherto been a frieze of more or less static figures confronting one another in profile became a perspective of living human beings reacting on one another and shaping their own destinies by the interplay of their contrasted characters. 'The purpose of Aeschylus is not, like that of other dramatists, to analyse the complex machinery of the human mind, but to reveal the relation in which men stand to the universal order of things' (Haigh, *Tragic Drama*). In other words, the typical Aeschylean play is essentially a narrative rather than a drama – a statement of what happened, rather than the presentation of a thing happening here and now to certain people who are what they are, and happening because they speak and act as their natures prompt them. So far as our evidence goes, Sophocles was the first to create that ever-exciting paradox of the theatre, in which, knowing perfectly well what *will* happen, we are yet absorbed in the contemplation of how and why it happens, and can watch it happening time and again as if new and unforeseen. If this is the secret of drama, its condition is that the persons of the drama should be free-willed creatures, not pawns in the hands of an omnipotent force or 'fate'. Sophoclean drama is the drama of living persons choosing their own paths to happiness or disillusion, to success, failure, or extinction.

June 1952   E. F. W.

AJAX

*

*

*The scene is before the tent of Ajax, in the camp of the Greeks near
    Troy.*
In the dim light of dawn, ODYSSEUS *is seen cautiously exploring
    the approach to the tent.* ATHENA, *a shadowy figure in the
    twilight, accosts him.*

ATHENA:
    Odysseus! What are you looking for? Still on the trail
    Of some advantage over your enemy?
    Yes, I have watched you, and I watch you now
    Here by the seaboard where the tent of Ajax
    Guards the furthest flank of the line; I see you,
    Doglike, nose to the ground, reading the tale
    Of his freshly printed traces, whither they lead,
    Inwards or out. You'll find him, if anyone will;

No Spartan hound has a keener scent for the chase.
He's there, the man you're looking for, his head
And hands sweating and blooded from the sword.
Leave peering and prying around the doors, and tell me
What is the purpose of your anxious search;
My knowledge can give you guidance.

ODYSSEUS: Athena's voice!
Ah, lovely goddess! Yes, it is your voice
Beyond a doubt, although I cannot see you;
I hear and know it and my heart leaps to meet it,
As to the summons of the clarion tongue
Of brazen trumpets. You have guessed right, my lady;
Ajax, he with the great shield, he is the man,
He is the man I am looking for. Last night
He played us a terrible trick; or someone did;
We're not sure yet, we're still groping in the dark.
I've made myself responsible for the search.
This morning we woke to find our sheep and cattle,
The whole of our booty, butchered in cold blood,
And the drovers dead beside them, every one.
We all think Ajax did it. Somebody saw him
Running wildly across the camp, alone,
With blood on his sword, and told me what he had seen.
I got on his tracks at once. Some of the footprints
Are clearly his, but some I'm not so sure of,
They might be anybody's. I'm glad you've come,
Goddess; you've been my pilot in days gone by,
And I shall still obey you.

ATHENA: Yes, Odysseus,
I know; and I lost no time in coming to meet you
To keep a watchful eye on your pursuit.

ODYSSEUS: Am I right then, lady, or am I wasting my time?

ATHENA: You are right. It was his work.

ODYSSEUS: What can have possessed him

To do such a senseless thing?

ATHENA: He was crazed with jealousy
For the armour of Achilles, which was given to you.

ODYSSEUS:
But why should he vent his anger upon the beasts?

ATHENA:
He thought he was dipping his hand in the blood of men.

ODYSSEUS:
His own compatriots? Was the onslaught aimed at us?

ATHENA: It was, and would have succeeded had I been idle.

ODYSSEUS: A daring stroke. How did he mean to do it?

ATHENA: Under cover of night he stole out alone to find you.

ODYSSEUS: And did he find us? Did he get close to us?

ATHENA: He did indeed; he got to the tent doors
Of Agamemnon and Menelaus.

ODYSSEUS: What held his hand
Back from the brink of slaughter?

ATHENA: It was I that baulked him
Of that fell triumph, darkening his vision
With a veil of phantasy, which overpowered him
So that he turned his wrath upon the cattle,
The sheep, and all the unassorted spoil
That the drovers had in charge. On this horned host
He dealt his death-blows, hacking and slaughtering
To right and left; to his deluded fancy
Now it was the sons of Atreus he was mauling
And butchering, now some other of your leaders,
Striking at each in turn. This way and that
He plunged like one demented; I was there
To goad and drive him deeper into the pit
Of black delusion; till at last he paused,
And taking the beasts for human prisoners,
Roped up the cattle that were still alive
And all the sheep, and marched them to his tent,

Where he is now tormenting them, like captives
Bound to the stake.
And now you too shall see
With your own eyes this hideous spectacle
And tell the Greeks.
Stay; do not be afraid.
He shall not harm you; I will keep his eyes
Averted from your face.

She calls to AJAX *within.*

You, sir, come out!
Stop trussing up your prisoners, and come out!
Ajax, come out, I say!

ODYSSEUS: Mercy, Athena!
Don't call him out.

ATHENA: Be quiet, and do not show yourself a coward.

ODYSSEUS: For pity's sake, let him remain inside.

ATHENA: Why should I? Was not this the man you knew?

ODYSSEUS: The man I hated, and I hate him still.

ATHENA: Now you can laugh at him; won't that content
you?

ODYSSEUS: I'd rather leave him where he is.

ATHENA: Afraid
To see a madman face to face?

ODYSSEUS: That's it.
I'd never fear him sane.

ATHENA: He will not see you,
However close you are.

ODYSSEUS: He still has eyes?

ATHENA: He has, but I will blind them.

ODYSSEUS: Be it so. Gods can do anything.

ATHENA: Don't move or speak.

ODYSSEUS: I'd better not. Would I were somewhere else.

ATHENA: Ajax! Do you hear me? Must I call again?
Is this the way you answer your protectress?

*AJAX appears, still possessed by madness, and holding a
blood-stained scourge in his hand.*

AJAX: Welcome, Athena! Daughter of Zeus, I greet you,
My faithful friend. You shall have golden offerings
To celebrate this victory.

ATHENA: Thank you, sir.
And is your sword well soaked in Grecian blood?

AJAX: Ay, that it is; and proud I am to say it.

ATHENA: You broke a lance with the two sons of Atreus?

AJAX: And once for all. Those two will never again
Insult the name of Ajax.

ATHENA: They are dead?

AJAX: Dead! Yes, they are dead. Now let them show me
Whether they'll take away my prize, my armour!

ATHENA: But what has happened to Laertes' son?
Have you let him escape?

AJAX: That crafty fox!
Do you want to know where he is?

ATHENA: Yes, where is Odysseus,
Your enemy of old?

AJAX: Ha, ha, my lady,
I've got him in the seat of honour, in there
Among my prisoners. I don't want him to die
Just yet.

ATHENA: What else will you do with him? What more
To add to your triumph?

AJAX: I'm going to tie him up
To a pillar in my private house.

ATHENA: Poor fellow!
What then?

AJAX: First whip him till he's black and blue;
Then kill him.

ATHENA: Must you torture the poor man so?

AJAX: Athena, in all but this your will commands me;
    His punishment cannot be changed.

ATHENA: Of course,
    Ajax, you must do exactly as you please.
    Leave nothing out.

AJAX: I'll go to work at once.
    And you be sure to back me up henceforward,
    And be my faithful ally, as before.

               He goes back into the tent.

ATHENA: And there you see the power of the gods,
    Odysseus. Is it not great? Here was a man
    Supreme in judgement, unsurpassed in action
    Matched to the hour. Did you ever know a better?

ODYSSEUS: Never. He was my enemy, but I'm sorry
    Now, with all my heart, for the misfortune
    Which holds him in its deadly grip. This touches
    My state as well as his. Are we not all,
    All living things, mere phantoms, shadows of nothing?

ATHENA: Therefore beware of uttering blasphemy
    Against the gods; beware of pride, puffed up
    By strength or substance. Know that all things mortal
    Hang in the scales; one day can tilt them up
    Or down. The gods love goodness, and abhor
    All that is evil.

      She vanishes. The CHORUS *of sailors approaches,*
             and ODYSSEUS *withdraws.*

CHORUS:
    To the Lord of the island fortress,
    To the Son of Telamon, king
    Of our seabound Salamis, hail!
    All's well with us, if well with you.
    But what if the hand of God
    Be heavy upon you, and angry tongues

Of clamorous Greeks beset you – then
Our hearts may jump, we are timorous doves
A-flutter with frightened eyes.

– Shameful tales were awake
Ere dawn was up, and a coil
About our ears: our master
Roaming the paddocks where the horses
Frisk their heels, and butchering
The captive herds, the unclaimed
War-spoil of the Greeks.

– A sword flashed in the darkness,
And beasts were slaughtered. Some such story
Odysseus tells with bated breath,
Whispering secret scandal
To credulous ears. Any tale he bears
Of you finds easy hearing now,
And the fun grows with the telling,
From mouth to mouth
The mocking laughter rises against you.

– That's it. Aim at the great
And you cannot miss. Tell a tale like that
Against me, and who would believe you? None.
Spite creeps in the path of the great ones.

– Ay, but where would the little be
Without the great, when it comes to saving
A city-wall?

– Little and great
Together, is best. The great do well
When the little are there to help them.

– Which is more than fools can understand,
Like those that clamour against you now;

And we are helpless to answer them,
Without our king.
The starlings flock and chatter
Behind your back; once show your face,
And we shall see them in that instant
Cowering, silent,
Under the vulture's eye.

'Tis a powerful tale they tell, and its offspring is shame
On all of us. Was it Artemis, daughter of Zeus,
Goddess who rides the Bull, driving our master
Into this raid on the cattle, the general property?
Was there some victory, and the price not paid,
Some glittering spoil or huntsmen's gift withheld?
Is that why the goddess is angry?
Or was it the Lord of War,
The Destroyer mailed in bronze who fights with us,
Paying some score of jealous pride
By dark devices in the night?

One thing is sure, this crazy escapade,
This raid on the beasts, was no sane man's intention.
If the gods come down to destroy the wits of a man,
Well, that's another matter. However it be,
May Zeus and Apollo save us from ugly scandal
Among the Greeks. O Ajax, for pity's sake,
While the great ones whisper against you
(Or that damned mischief-maker,
The spawn of Sisyphus), you must not stay
Hidden here in the tents by the sea,
Or you lose your name for ever.

Come, why are you sitting
This long time
So far from the fighting,

Feeding a blaze
Of hate that rises
High in the sky?
Malice and hatred
Walk unhindered
In open country,
And loud tongues jangle
In angry chorus –
  O the pity, the pity,
  'Tis more than we can bear.

TECMESSA *comes out of the tent.*

TECMESSA: Shipmates of Ajax,
  Sons of Erechtheid soil,
  Sadness is here for all that love
  The house of Telamon, that lies so far,
  So far away.
  Ajax our lord, our strength, our rock, lies fallen,
  His mightiness brought low, his light
  Darkened with clouds of woe.

CHORUS: This night has capped the day
  With heavier trouble, then?
  What can that be? What more?
  You, daughter of the Phrygian Teleutas,
  Have all our master's love,
  Bride of his battle-spear;
  Tell us what more you know.

TECMESSA: How can I tell it? There are no words
  To describe this deathlike thing.
  Our noble master is mad; Ajax struck blind
  With madness in the night.
  Look into the tent and see
  His offerings, his victims bleeding,
  His handiwork.

CHORUS: It is plain. There is no escaping
    From the awful thing you are telling.
    His soul is a fire; and the story
    Is loud in the mouths of the people,
    And grows on their powerful tongues
    To a mighty clamour.
    I fear what is coming upon us.
    He is branded with shame and marked for death,
    If indeed it was his misguided hand,
    His sword in the dark, that killed
    Those beasts and the watchers of herds and horses.

TECMESSA: O then it is true! It was there he took
    His prisoners, and brought them back,
    A herd of captives. He brought them in,
    He shed their blood on the ground,
    He tore them limb from limb.
    There were two white-footed rams he seized,
    Cut off the head of one, tore out its tongue,
    And flung them down;
    Then tied the other to a post
    Upright, and flogged it with a scourge
    Of double harness-rein that sang
    As the blows fell; while he cursed
    With words no mortal power
    Put in his mouth to speak.

CHORUS: There is nothing else but to cover
    Our heads and creep away, then.
    Or quickly back to the oar-bench
    And pull for the sea, for safety
    From the wash of the angry vengeance
    Of our two leaders,
    The sons of Atreus. Stoning
    Is the death they'll have in store for us;
    I have no stomach for that encounter;

To die at our master's side —
No, his is a fate that asks no sharing.

TECMESSA: But wait. The storm is over,
The lightning past, like the southern gale
When its first sharp rage is spent.
He understands; but now there is other pain
That he must bear, the bitter torment
Of seeing his own hand's mischief,
The guilt that none can share.

CHORUS: If the worst is over, all may yet be well.
What's past is soon forgotten.

TECMESSA: Which would you choose,
If you had the choice; to enjoy a pleasure yourself
At the cost of another's pain, or both alike
To share a trouble?

CHORUS: I would say, my lady,
Two troubles must be worse than one.

TECMESSA: So now
The end of his malady is not the end
Of our afflictions.

CHORUS: How is that, my lady?
That's hard to see.

TECMESSA: While Ajax was distraught,
He at least found happiness in his obsession;
We, sane, were pained to see him. Now he is well,
And free of the sickness, bitter grief torments him,
And ours is none the less. Are there not here
Two troubles in place of one?

CHORUS: Indeed there are.
I fear some god has laid a hand on him.
It must be so, if, when the fit is over,
He is yet no happier than while it raged.

TECMESSA: It is so, there's no denying.

CHORUS: We grieve with you.

How did the trouble first descend on him?
Will you tell us what happened?
TECMESSA: You shall hear all that happened,
　As if you saw it.
　　　At the turn of midnight,
The last late lamp put out, Ajax arose,
Took up a two-edged sword, and started away
On some blind impulse. I called out to him,
'What is the matter, Ajax? There has been no trumpet
Or message for you; what are you going to do?
The camp's asleep.' 'Woman,' he answered shortly,
'Women should be seen, not heard.' – the old, old story!
I kept obedient silence, and out he went
Alone. What passion then came over him
I cannot say. Soon he was back again
With a leash of cattle roped like prisoners,
Oxen, and sheepdogs with their woolly charges.
Then he began to slaughter them, beheading,
Slitting the upturned throat, cleaving the nape;
Or left them bound and savagely attacked them,
Tormenting them like human captives. Then
He turned and darted swiftly through the door
To parley with some phantom, talking wildly
Against the Atreidae – and something about Odysseus –
With shouts of mocking laughter about his triumph
And the trick he had served them in this escapade.
Then he came stumbling back into the hut
And slowly, painfully, regained his senses.
Looking about him at the scene of havoc
That filled the hut, he uttered a loud cry
And beat his brow, and tumbling to the ground
Over the tumbled carcases that strewed
The sheep-shambles, sat there with clutching fingers
Gripping his hair – sat for a long time silent.

At last he challenged me – and with what threats –
To tell him all that had happened, where he was
And how he came there. I was afraid, my friends,
And told him everything I knew. At that
He broke into such piteous cries of anguish
As I had never heard him use before;
For he had always taught me that loud crying
Was only fit for cowards and mollycoddles;
If he lamented it was with low moans,
A bull's deep groaning – never a shrill complaint.
And so he still sits, utterly dejected;
Will take no food nor drink, but only sits
Still where he fell among the slaughtered beasts.
He clearly means to do some dreadful thing,
If there is any meaning in his words,
His bitter cries.

    O friends, come in and help me –
I am here only to ask you this – come in
And help me if you can. In such a case
A friendly word may be the sovereign remedy.

CHORUS: This is sad news, my lady. To think our master
  Should be so terribly bewitched.

AJAX (*within*): O! O!...

TECMESSA:
  We have not seen the worst. Do you hear him now?
  How he groans!

AJAX: O! O!...

CHORUS: Is he still afflicted
  Or suffering at the sight of what he did
  When the rage was on him?

AJAX: O my son, my son!

TECMESSA: He calls for his son Eurysaces. Ah why?
  Eurysaces, where are you?... O what shall I do?

AJAX: Teucer!... Where's Teucer?... Has he gone for ever

A-plundering, while I sit dying here?

CHORUS: I do not think he is mad. Open the door, there!
He may perhaps be calmer when he sees us.

TECMESSA: I'll open it ... Look in, and you shall see
The work of his hands, and how it is with him.

*She opens the door; AJAX is seen sitting among
the slaughtered beasts.*

AJAX: Good shipmates, my only friends,
My only loyal comrades.
The storm has broken over my head,
I am tempest-tossed and drowned
In a sea of blood.

CHORUS (*to* TECMESSA):
Ay, then, you told us nothing but the truth.
It's plain he is still disordered in his mind.

AJAX: Ho there!
My trusty mariners,
Who came aboard with me
To sweep the sea with flashing blades!
No one but you can help me out of this —
No one but you —
Come, make an end of me
And let my carcase lie here too.

CHORUS: No, God forbid, sir. Evil cannot be cured
By other evil; you only give yourself
Worse pain to bear by thinking so.

AJAX: Here is the bold, the strong,
The fearless fighter in the line!
See his brave handiwork
Among these innocent dumb beasts,
And laugh, laugh at his shame!

TECMESSA: Ajax, my lord, you must not say such things.

AJAX: Away with you! Out of my sight!
O! O! ...

CHORUS: For the love of God, sir, listen and be advised.
AJAX: That I should be so cursed!
  The devils, I had them in my hand
  And let them go!
  I let them go, and turned aside
  To spill the rich red blood
  Of these fine creatures.
CHORUS: Do not torment yourself for what is past.
  What's done cannot be undone.
AJAX: Where is Odysseus now,
  That sharp-eyed instrument
  Of all ill-doing, he,
  The vilest creature in all our camp,
  Shall he laugh at me now?
CHORUS: Laughter or tears, 'tis God that sends them to us.
AJAX: I'd meet him now, broken as I am ...
  Ay, now!
CHORUS: Be calm, sir. You are in no plight to boast.
AJAX: That vile smooth villain, O
  Zeus, O father of my fathers,
  Let me but kill
  That fox, and those two brother-kings
  Who lord it over us –
  Kill them and die!
CHORUS: Nay, if you pray for death, pray too for mine.
  I could not live without you.
AJAX: O darkness that is my light,
  O night of death, my only day,
  Take me, take me, I pray,
  Into your house for ever. I have no hope
  Of mercy from the gods, I am not worthy
  To ask the help of man.
  One irresistible
  Daughter of Zeus

Hunts me to death.
And how should man escape that enemy?
Where should I hide,
Now that my day is over, and revenge
Barks at my heels?
Here are the triumphs of my folly
There my armed comrades wait
To take my life.
TECMESSA: How can I bear it? How could so good a man
  Be brought to such despair?
AJAX: Roads of the tossing sea,
  Water-meadows and wave-washed rocks,
  I have been too long among you,
  Too long at Troy. You will not see me again –
  Not see me alive. Ay, mark this, everyone –
  You will not see me again.
  Never again,
  Friendly Scamander,
  River we love!
  This is the last of Ajax, such a man –
  Yes, let me boast –
  A man whose equal Troy has never seen
  All of the men
  That ever left the shores of Greece.
  Now see him: here he sits
  A man disgraced.
CHORUS: You must not speak so; yet you must; can I
  Forbid or suffer you, fallen so low?
AJAX: Aias! Aias!
  How fit a name to weep with! Who could have known
  How well those syllables would spell my story?
  Aias! Alas! Over and over again
  I cry Alas! How am I fallen!
  My father won the army's first rewards

Here on this soil of Ida, and brought home
A prize of beauty and an honoured name
For valour. I, his son, came, strong as he,
To this same ground, and bore as brave a part
In action, and am now brought down to this,
Death, and disgrace among my countrymen.
One thing is certain – had Achilles lived
To name the champion worthiest to receive
His weapons in reward for valiant service,
They never would have fallen to other hands
Than mine. Instead of that, these sons of Atreus
Have filched them from me for a scheming rascal
And turned their backs on me and all my triumphs.
They'd not have lived to rig another verdict
Against a man; I would have seen to that,
Had not my eyes deceived me and my brain
Wheeled wide of my intention. I was foiled,
At the very instant when I raised my hand
To strike them, by the undefeatable,
The hard-eyed daughter of Zeus; she sent the plague
Of madness on me; and the blood of beasts
Is this that dyes my hands. *They* have escaped,
And laugh! It was not my doing. Little men,
When gods work mischief, may escape their betters.

   And now what must I do? Hated of gods,
Hated of all the Greeks, hated of Troy,
And of this very soil – must I go home
Across the Aegean sea, and leave these shiproads,
And leave the Atreidae to their own devices?
How shall I meet my father, Telamon,
When I come there? How will he welcome me
When I come empty-handed, with no prize
To match the crown of honours that he wore?
I cannot do it.

Shall I go to Troy?
And storm her fortress, single against them all,
And die in one last action of renown?
No; that would be too kind to the Atreidae;
That's not the way.
    What can I do? Some feat
To make my poor old father understand
He has no soft-bellied coward for a son.
Long life? Who but a coward would ask for it,
Beset by endless evil? Can he enjoy
Counting the days that pass; now a step forward,
Now a step backward, on the way to death?
Who'd be that man? To huddle over the coals
Of flickering hope. Not I. Honour in life,
Or honour in death; there is no other thing
A nobleman can ask for. That is all.

CHORUS: Ajax, none can deny you have spoken frankly
And like your true self. Yet do not be hasty;
Forget these bitter thoughts, and let your friends
Win your submission.

TECMESSA: Ajax, O my lord!
(O how mankind is cursed by Fate's hard law!)
My father was a free and happy man,
A power among the Phrygians. What am I?
A slave. Say that it was the will of heaven;
But your hand did it. Well, let it be so;
I am your consort, and I wish you well;
And I beseech you by the God we worship
As man and wife, the bed you brought me to,
Do not consign me to the cruel taunts
Of those that hate you, and the horrid hands
Of my next master. On the day you die,
And dying leave me helpless, think of me
That same day roughly carried off by Greeks –

Your son too – to a life of slavery.
Think of the stinging insults aimed at me
By some new owner: 'Look! Whom have we here?
Ajax's woman – Ajax, the army's hero –
O what a fall, from such felicity
To such subjection!' Can't you hear them say it?
The blow will fall on me – but on your head,
And on your blood, will fall the shame of it.
O Ajax, have you the heart to leave your father
To face old age without you? Have you the heart
To leave your mother a long legacy
Of lonely years? Think how she prays and prays
To have you home alive. Think of your son,
Your son, my lord; must he be left defenceless,
So young, without you, under heartless guardians?
Can you do such a thing to him, and me?
Whom have I left but you? Where can I go?
Your sword has made my home a desert. My mother,
My father, by another stroke of fate,
Were gathered into the house of death. What land,
When you are gone, will ever be home for me,
What fortune bring me joy? You are my all.
Have you forgotten me? Can any man
Forget what happiness has once been his?
Love must breed love. Not to remember kindness
Is to be called no longer noble.

CHORUS: O Ajax, can you not pity her, as I do?
Can you not say she is right?

AJAX: I'll say she is right
Only when she can show she is obedient.

TECMESSA: I will do anything you ask, dear Ajax.

AJAX: Bring my son here to me. I want to see him.

TECMESSA:
O, I was afraid – I sent him out of the way.

AJAX: You mean, when I was ... in trouble – is that what
    you mean?

TECMESSA:
    Yes – thinking he might meet you ... and be killed.

AJAX: That would have been a pretty piece of justice.

TECMESSA: I took good care it shouldn't happen.

AJAX: Well done.
    You showed good judgement.

TECMESSA: How can I help you now?

AJAX: I want him here.
    I want to see him and speak to him myself.

TECMESSA: You shall. He is with the guards, not far away.

AJAX: Let him come here at once.

TECMESSA: Eurysaces! ...
    Your father wants you ... One of you, bring him here.
    Whichever of you is looking after him ...

AJAX: Is he coming? Or can't he hear you?

TECMESSA: Yes, he's coming ...
    One of the guards is bringing him.

AJAX: That's right ...
    Bring him into my arms ... No son of mine, I hope,
    Is frightened by the sight of fresh-drawn blood.
    It'll soon be time to break him in and train him
    In the hard school where his father learnt. My son,
    May you be everything your father was,
    But less unfortunate. Then you will do well.
    I would give much to be in your place now,
    Seeing this trouble and not understanding
    All that it means. There is no time of life
    So happy as the days of innocence
    Before you know what joy or sorrow are.
    But when you come to know it, then, my son,
    See that your enemies know whose son you are.

Till then, feed on the bubble air, enjoy
Your little life, and make your mother happy.
You will be in safe hands, even when I am gone.
There's not a Greek will dare to lift a finger
To hurt or shame you; the ever-faithful Teucer,
Whom I shall leave to be your guardian,
Will give his all in your behalf, unsparing,
When he returns from business with the enemy
Which keeps him from us now.
And you, my men,
My fellow soldiers and sailors, you have a share
In this obligation; tell Teucer this from me –
To take the lad back home to my father's house,
That he and my mother may have him for a son
To comfort their remaining years. My armour –
Tell Teucer this – is not for any umpire
(And least of all that enemy of mine)
To parcel out among the Greeks. Look, son;
This broad shield bears your name, EURYSACES –
Seven thicknesses, proof against any spear –
The hand-strap firmly stitched. Learn how to hold it . . .
There . . . it is yours. But all my other weapons
I will have with me in the grave . . .
Tecmessa,
Take him away with you, and shut your doors.
Women must weep, but let there be no weeping
This side the threshold. Quick, out of my sight!
Dirges and canticles are no prescription
For ills that need the knife.

CHORUS: You're resolute, sir,
And sorry I am to hear it. This sharp speaking
Has an ill sound.

TECMESSA: O Ajax, O my lord,
What do you mean to do?

AJAX: Ask me no questions.
   Possess yourself in patience.
TECMESSA: I am afraid.
   O for the gods' sake, for your own son's sake,
   Do not desert us!
AJAX: I cannot listen to you.
   Do you believe I still owe any duty
   Or service to the gods?
TECMESSA: That's blasphemy.
AJAX: What of it?
TECMESSA: Will you not listen?
AJAX: I've listened to more than enough.
TECMESSA: My lord, I am frightened.
AJAX: Close the doors, I say!
TECMESSA: Have pity, have pity!
AJAX: You're a fool, Tecmessa,
   To think that I could change my nature now
   On your instructions.

The doors are closed, shutting AJAX *from sight.*

CHORUS:
   O glorious Salamis, beauty of the world
   Set fast for ever in the washing waves,
   Pity us here,
   Stretched on our grassy beds. How long?
   Months without number,
   Year after weary year,
   Waiting for nothing but our cold
   Dark everlasting graves.

   Ajax, your champion, whom you sent away
   So valorous, lies here, a sorry sight,
   Brooding alone,
   Cribbed with a sickness of the mind

Past human cure,
The great things he has done
Forgotten; such deeds our kings repay
With unforgiving spite.

His white-haired mother, numbering old days
Of many years gone by,
Will hear of this calamity,
This malady that eats his soul away,
And then, O pity, pity,
Who will bear
To hear her crying –
Not as the nightingale
With soft complaining,
But with loud wail
Of woe – and see her there
Drumming her breast,
Tumbling her snow-white hair?

It is better that death should take a man diseased
And wandering in the maze
Of madness – born to be the best
Of all the warring Greeks, now gone adrift
Out of his course, and lost
In strange uncharted ways.
How will his father hear
Of this undoing –
How will they tell
The unhappy sire
Of such vile shame
As yet befell
No other of his name?

　　　　　AJAX *comes out of the tent; his mood is now*
　　　　　　　　　calm and resolute.

AJAX:

The long unmeasured pulse of time moves everything.
There is nothing hidden that it cannot bring to light,
Nothing once known that may not become unknown.
Nothing is impossible. The most sacred oath
Is fallible; a will of iron may bend.
A little while ago, I was tough-tempered
As the hardest iron; but now my edge is blunted
By a woman's soft persuasion. I am loth
To leave a widow and a fatherless child
Here among enemies. This is what I must do:
I must go down to the meadows by the sea
And wash till I am clean of all this filth,
So that the Goddess may withhold her wrath
And spare me. I will take this sword of mine,
My adversary, to some secret place
And hide it, bury it out of sight for ever,
Consigned to death and darkness. It was Hector's,
My deadliest enemy's gift, and since I had it
The Greeks have done me nothing but ill. How true
The saying is, it is always dangerous
To touch an enemy's gifts. I have learned my lesson,
To obey the gods – and not be disrespectful
To the sons of Atreus; they are in command,
And we are under them; that is as it should be.
There is no power so sacred, none so strong
As to defy all rank and precedence.
The snowy feet of Winter walk away
Before ripe Summer; and patrolling Night
Breaks off her rounds to let the Dawn ride in
On silver horses lighting up the sky.
The winds abate and leave the groaning sea
To sleep awhile. Even omnipotent Sleep
Locks and unlocks his doors and cannot hold

His prisoners bound for ever. Must not we
Learn this self-discipline? I think we must.
I now know this, that while I hate my enemy
I must remember that the time may come
When he will be my friend; as, loving my friend
And doing him service, I shall not forget
That he one day may be my enemy.
Friendship is but a treacherous anchorage,
As most men know ... Well, never mind ...
Tecmessa,
You must go in, and ask the blessed gods
To grant me all my heart's desire. (*She goes.*)
And you,
My friends, to help me, join your prayers with hers.
Ask Teucer, when he comes, to see to things
As I would wish, and to look after you.
Do this for me. I must be on my way.
When next you hear of me, I shall be safe,
And all this suffering ended.
                                        Exit.

CHORUS:
   Now I could jump for joy,
   Now I could fly
   Light as a bird. O Pan, O Pan,
   O revelling Prince whom the great gods follow,
   Come from the rocky height,
   Come from Cyllene's white
   Snow-crest, dance over the sea;
   Let Nysian mode inspire,
   And Cnosian measures, our fancy free.
   Dance, dance to our heart's desire.
   From Delos, from the Icarian shore,
   Come near, Apollo,
   And be with us for evermore

Darkness of horror and shame
Is lifted away,
Tempest of blood
Washed from the sky.
Praise be to Zeus, sun shines again
On our swift sea-rovers, now
Ajax is well and goes to pay
His vows to heaven, devout
And reverent, all his pain purged out
By all-destroying time.
Nothing is past belief, if now the wild
Fury of enmity is mended,
Ajax and the Atreidae reconciled
And passion ended.

A MESSENGER *arrives from the Greek camp.*

MESSENGER: News, friends!
Teucer is back from his raid in the Mysian hills,
And all the Grecian army in an uproar.
They heard he was on the way, and when he reached
The generals' quarters, there were crowds about him
All howling at him in an angry chorus.
'The maniac's brother', 'the traitor's brother', they called
him;
Nothing would do but he must be stoned to death
And torn to pieces. And it went so far,
Hands flew to hilts and blades were ripped from scabbards;
Till, in the nick of time, the intervention
Of elder voices settled the dispute.
But news must go to the proper ears. Where's Ajax?
Ajax must hear of this.
CHORUS: He is not here.
He went away a little while ago,

A new man, and intent on some new business.

MESSENGER: Ill luck! The man that sent me on this errand
Sent me too late – or I have been too slow.

CHORUS: What errand? What's the matter?

MESSENGER: Teucer said
On no account must Ajax be allowed
To stir out of his tent, until he came.

CHORUS: Well, out he's gone, and for the best of reasons –
To make his peace with heaven.

MESSENGER: That makes no sense,
If we trust Calchas and his prophecy!

CHORUS: What prophecy? What more do you know of this?

MESSENGER:
I know what I saw. The leaders were in council;
Calchas was there, and soon he left his place
And went to speak to Teucer, out of earshot
Of Menelaus and Agamemnon; took his hand
In a friendly grip, and begged him earnestly
By hook or crook to keep Ajax at home,
Not let him out of sight this whole day long,
Or else he'd never see him alive again.
For on this day, no other, he was doomed
To meet Athena's wrath. For, said the prophet,
The gods have dreadful penalties in store
For worthless and redundant creatures, mortals
Who break the bounds of mortal modesty.
And Ajax showed he had no self-control
The day he left his home. 'Son,' said his father –
And very properly – 'Go out to win,
But win with God beside you.' 'Oh,' said Ajax
With vain bravado, 'any fool can win
With God beside him; I intend to win
Glory and honour on my own account.'
A terrible boast. And then another time

Divine Athena came to urge him on
And told him where to lay about his enemies;
He answered blasphemously 'Holy One,
Give your assistance to some other Greeks;
The line won't break where I am in command.'
This kind of talk it was that broke the bounds
Of mortal modesty; and his reward
Was the full fury of Athena's anger.
But if he lives today, there is a chance
We may yet save him, with the help of heaven.

   When Calchas told him this, Teucer at once
Called me to where he sat, and sent me off
With these instructions for you. If we've lost him,
Ajax has not an hour to live, or Calchas
Is no true prophet.

CHORUS: Tecmessa! There's bad news.
 A messenger is here.
 O poor Tecmessa!
 'Tis touch and go for all of us, this business.

Enter TECMESSA, *with* EURYSACES

TECMESSA:What now? Must you disturb my rest again?
 I thought this was the end of all my troubles.

CHORUS: Listen to this man's news; bad news, I'm afraid,
 Of Ajax.

TECMESSA: What, sir? Is there danger still?

MESSENGER: As to yourself, madam, I cannot say.
 Ajax may be in mortal danger, though,
 If he has left his tent.

TECMESSA: He has, he has.
 O sir, why, what's your message?

MESSENGER: Orders from Teucer
 To keep your husband strictly in his tent,
 Not let him venture out alone this day.

TECMESSA:
  Teucer? Where is he? Why has he sent this order?
MESSENGER:
  He has just returned to camp; and has good reason
  To think that mortal peril threatens Ajax
  If once he leaves this place.
TECMESSA: Alas the day!
  How did you find this out?
MESSENGER: The prophet Calchas,
  The son of Thestor, warned him of it; this day
  Brings life or death for Ajax.
TECMESSA: O my friends,
  Avert the fate that threatens me! Go quickly,
  Fetch Teucer here at once! Some of you, search
  The beaches, east and west, search every way
  Where my unhappy husband may have gone!
  The wretched man deceived me after all!
  It's plain he does not love me any longer.
  O child, what shall I do? We must do something.
  I'll go myself as far as I can. Make haste!
  We have no time to lose, if we're to save
  A man in search of death.
CHORUS: I'm with you, madam,
  And good as my word. I'll do what's to be done,
  As fast as feet can carry me.
                    They hurry out in all directions.

After a brief interval, AJAX *appears. He has now selected the place
  of his death, and kneeling down he plants his sword by the hilt
  in the earth, fixing it firmly with careful deliberation.*
AJAX: There. Now he's ready. The executioner
  Stands ready for his business. He'll not fail.
  Why should he? – now I come to think of it.
  That sword was Hector's; he was the man I hated

And loathed the sight of, more than any I knew;
And here it stands, in the grip of the soil of Troy,
Enemy soil. The edge is new, the stone
Has eaten the iron clean. And I've taken care
To fix it firmly so that there'll be no bungling,
Only a swift and kindly death.
There, then; we're ready.
Next, my prayers:
O Zeus, to thee above all, as I am bound,
I pray for succour. It is not much I ask.
Only that thou wilt send some messenger
To break this news to Teucer, so that he
May be the first to find me lying here
On this wet sword, and lift me in his arms,
Before some one of those I hate can get me
And throw me to the dogs and carrion crows.
Zeus, grant me this.
And this: when I thrust the sword
Through to my heart, may Hermes guide my way
Under the earth, and lay me down to sleep,
In one swift easy jump from life to death.
And this prayer too:
May the ever-living Maidens
Who watch for ever the sufferings of men,
The stern unresting Furies, see this death
And know that the sons of Atreus brought it on me:
And wipe them utterly out with deaths as vile
As their vile selves. Go to it, you swift avengers;
Drink deep, and spare not one of all their people!
And you, that ride the high ways of the heavens,
Great Sun,
Pull up your golden-harnessed horses
Over my native land, and tell this story
Of death and ruin to my aged father

And to my sorrowing mother. She will weep,
How she will weep, and fill the streets with weeping,
Unhappy mother, when she hears of this.
But now there is no time for tears. To work,
To work, and quickly. Death, O Death, come now
And look upon me. We shall meet again,
And I shall greet you in the other world.
But this bright day, this chariot of the sky,
I shall not see again. Farewell for ever,
Light; and Salamis, dear sacred land,
Dear homestead; and great Athens too, farewell,
Whose folk are kin to mine; farewell this Troy,
These fields and rivers, my bread and water; now
Ajax salutes you once, and speaks no more
Upon this earth.

> *He throws himself upon the sword, and dies.*
> *There is a short interval of silence.*

The CHORUS *are heard approaching; half of them come into view on one side of the stage; they do not yet see the body of* AJAX.

CHORUS 1: Well, trouble take and trouble make.
　We've searched the country high and low
　And not a thing to show –
　What ho! Who's there? Surely I heard a sound –
CHORUS 2 (*approaching from the other side*): Ahoy, shipmates!
CHORUS 1: What news?
CHORUS 2: We've covered every inch of ground
　To westward of the ships.
CHORUS 1: And found?
CHORUS 2: Found heavy going, nothing more
　Of what we're looking for.
CHORUS 1: We too; no sign
　Or trace of him along the eastward line.

(Severally)
Some fisherman now
With eyes awake
On his weary work
Might give us a clue –

Or a water-sprite
Of the Hellespont,
Or a nymph from Mount
Olympus' height –

Such only could say
If our wandering lord
In his restless mood
Had come this way –

'Tis a shame to us all
If we can't make shift
To overhaul
Our master adrift –

　　　Meanwhile TECMESSA *has reached the place where*
　　　　　　AJAX *lies, and is heard lamenting.*

TECMESSA: Ah me, ah me!
CHORUS: What cry was that? In the wood. Who's there?
TECMESSA: Alas, alas!
CHORUS: It is poor Tecmessa, his captive-wife,
　　Dissolved in grief.
　　　　　　　　　　　They turn towards her.
TECMESSA: Alas, my friends,
　　There is nothing left for me to live for.
CHORUS: Why, what has happened?
TECMESSA: Here is Ajax,
　　Dead, and the sword still sunk in his heart.
CHORUS: Dead! O master, master! This is the end,
　　The end of our homeward sailing,

Ay, death for all of us
Your shipmates, and your broken-hearted lady.
TECMESSA: We can do nothing for him
But weep, weep for his passing.
CHORUS: Who can have lent a hand
To help him to this awful end?
TECMESSA: No other but himself. Look, here is the witness,
The sword fixed in the ground, on which he fell.
CHORUS: Shed his own blood, O God,
And we – fools that we were
To let him out of our sight –
Knew nothing of it, O blind
And dull of wit. So dies
A wilful man, doomed Ajax. Show us,
Show us where Ajax lies.
TECMESSA: No one shall see. This cloak shall be his pall.
No one that loved him could endure this sight –
The crimson fountain gushing from the wound
His own hand made, and welling through the nostrils.
What shall I do? O Ajax, who is there now
To lift you in loving arms? Who but your brother
Should lay you in your grave? O where is Teucer?
Ajax, my Ajax, to have come to this –
Even your enemies must shed their tears
To see you fallen so.
CHORUS: It had to be;
That stubborn soul
Was doomed to its dole
Of misery;

Early and late
That venomous tongue
Of wrath had sung
Its hymn of hate,

Its clamorous curse
On the Atreid kings.
These sufferings
Sprang from their source

That pregnant day
When a sword became
The prize in a game
Of bravery.

TECMESSA: Alas, alas!

CHORUS: Her heart must break. 'Tis a noble grief.

TECMESSA: Ah me, ah me!

CHORUS: Weep, my lady, and weep again.
You have good reason; he you have lost
Had loved you well.

TECMESSA: Well you may think – how well I know,
Alas, too well.

CHORUS: Ay, truly.

TECMESSA: And O my little son, what harness now
Shall bow our necks, what eyes watch over us?

CHORUS: Speak not of that: the brother-kings
Will have no pity. Only tears
Can tell what cruelty is in those hands.
God keep it from you.

TECMESSA: Was it not God
That brought it on us?

CHORUS: Truly his hand
Was heavily laid upon you.

TECMESSA: Pallas Athene,
The tyrannous daughter of Zeus, conceived this outrage
To please Odysseus.

CHORUS: The 'much-enduring man'
Will laugh to his black heart's content
Over this tragic tale of madness.

How he will laugh – O cruelty! –
Telling the tale to the brother-kings,
The sons of Atreus.

TECMESSA:
Well, let them laugh, and mock their enemy's downfall.
A time will come for them to mourn his loss,
Though they despised him living – the time will come
In a turning-point of battle. Witless fools
Know not their own advantage till they lose it.
His death can bring no joy to them, to me
Nothing but bitter grief; but he lies happy.
All he desired was death of his own choosing,
And that he has. What right have they to laugh?
He died in the hands of God, not theirs, not theirs.
Find triumph in that, Odysseus, if you can!
Ajax is lost to them, and I am left
To mourn his going.

CHORUS: Hush now. I think I hear a voice. 'Tis Teucer,
And surely it is for this calamity
He cries so loudly.

Enter TEUCER.

TEUCER: Ajax! O my brother,
My brother ... that dear face ... O is it true,
And are you ... as they told me?

CHORUS: He is dead, sir.

TEUCER: O great misfortune!

CHORUS: It is so indeed.

TEUCER: How shall I bear this heavy stroke?

CHORUS: Ay, heavy,
Heavy in truth.

TEUCER: Sad, sad ... But what of the child,
His child? He must be somewhere in the land.

CHORUS: We left him by the tents.

TEUCER: Fetch him at once;

At once, before he fall into the hands
That wait to snatch the lion's whelp away
When parted from its dam. Lose not a moment.
Go with her, you. Few can resist the chance
Of scoring off a fallen adversary.

TECMESSA *goes, with one of the soldiers.*

CHORUS: Ay, now I think of it, Ajax before he died
Expressed the wish that you should take the child
Under your care; as you are doing now.

TEUCER: O Ajax, Ajax! When did I ever see
So sorrowful a sight? Was any road
More galling to my soul than that which brought me
Questing upon your tracks to find you here
Fallen, as I had feared? Rumour was rife
About the camp, clear as a voice from heaven,
That you were dead. I heard, and even then
Could well have wept; but now that I have seen,
My heart is broken . . .
Uncover him; let me see everything,
However horrible . . .
Grim sight . . . And O what ruthless hardihood!
So rich a seed of sorrow planted here,
Which I must reap. Where on this mortal earth
Shall I go now, who failed you in your need?
What sort of welcome waits for me at home
When I go back without you? Can you see
The happy smile upon our father's face?
Poor Telamon – as if he ever smiled
Even at good news! Now what names he'll call me –
He'll have no mercy on me – bastard brat
Of a captive concubine, coward and weakling
That like a traitor let his brother die
(The brother I loved!) or did it for a trick
To step into a dead man's shoes. All that

He'll fling at me in the ungoverned wrath
His age is burdened with; no straw's too light
To give him cause for quarrel. I shall be branded
A slave, an outlaw – it will come to that –
Disowned and driven out. Such is the greeting
I may expect at home. While here in Troy
Dangers abound, and I am well-nigh helpless.
Your death has left me thus. What can I do? . . .
O brother . . . let me see if I can lift you
Free of that ghastly blade which gleams there still,
The evident destroyer of your life . . .

*(He extricates the sword, and holds it in his hand
recognizing it.)*

You see, it had to be Hector after all
That did this thing, although he died before you.
By heaven, what a fate has bound these two
Together! The girdle Ajax gave to Hector
Became the rope that lashed him to the chariot
And dragged him to his death. Now Hector's sword,
His gift to Ajax, has laid Ajax low.
Who but some Fury could have forged the sword,
What cruel craftsman but the God of Death
Devised the girdle? These, like all things ever,
I must believe are engines of the gods
Designed against mankind. If this be error,
Then he who thinks it so must go his way
As I go mine.

CHORUS: Sir, you have said enough.
'Tis time to think of your brother's burial,
And with what answer you will meet the enemy
Who comes, I see, and comes, no doubt, to mock
At our misfortunes, like the knave he is.

TEUCER: One of our people? Who is it you see?

CHORUS:

Menelaus, the man for whom we made this voyage.

TEUCER: Ah yes — there's no mistaking *his* approach.

Some of the men stoop to raise the body.

Enter MENELAUS, *with one or more attendants.*

MENELAUS: You there, I forbid you to lift up that body,
Or lay a finger on it. Leave it where it lies.

TEUCER:

What right have you to give them such an order?

MENELAUS: It is my wish, and the wish of our commander.

TEUCER: And may we know your reason?

MENELAUS: This is the reason.

We brought this man from Greece, thinking we brought
An ally and a friend to Greeks; instead
What did we find him? A more dangerous foe
Than any Trojan; plotting the sheer destruction
Of all our army, stealing a march on us
At dead of night, to put us all to the sword.
Had it not been for some good god, who nipped
That venture in the bud, we should be lying
As dead as he; his doom would have been ours,
And he would be alive. But, as it happened,
The god drew off the assault, so that it fell
Upon our sheep and cattle. That is why
We say no man alive shall have the power
To put this body in a grave. We'll throw him
Out on the yellow sand, and let the sea-birds
Feed on his carcase. — Keep your anger in! —
We couldn't rule him while he lived; but dead,
Say what you will, we'll keep him in subjection
Under our hands; he never in his life
Obeyed a word of mine. When common men
Dare to defy the powers set over them,
They show their evil nature. There is no law

In a city where there is no fear, no order
In any camp that is not fenced about
With discipline and respect. The strongest man
Must be prepared to fall, it may be, at a touch
Of small mischance. In fear and modesty
He has the surest shield; where licence reigns,
And insolence, the ship of state is doomed,
However fair her course at first, to plunge
To bottomless disaster. Fear, I say,
Should have its proper place; let us not think
That if we please ourselves we can escape
Paying the price of pleasure with our pains.
Our turn will come. This was a man once proud
And full of fire; now I'm the one to boast.
And this I warn you: take no hand or part
In burying him; for if you do, your grave
Will soon be ready for you.

CHORUS: Sir, your precepts
Are true and wise; but should you not beware
Of outrage on the dead?

TEUCER: O my good friends,
What wonder if a man of humble origin
Should act in error, when the so-called noble
Can speak so falsely.
(*To* MENELAUS) Come, let's have it plain:
You say *you* brought him here, *you* found an ally
To help the Greeks? It was his own will brought him.
He owned no other master. Who made you
His officer? Who put you in command
Of those whom Ajax brought from home, his people?
You came as Sparta's king, not ours. What title
Had you to give him orders? None; no more
Than he to govern you. You were not even
Supreme commander of this enterprise,

But under orders too; you had no right
To give commands to Ajax. Keep your orders
For those that follow you, and your rough tongue
For their chastisement. I will bury my brother
As piety demands; I do not fear
You or your brother-chief, say what you will.
It was never on your precious wife's account
That Ajax took up arms, like the poor slaves
Who toil beneath your yoke; he had an oath
That bound him to this task, no thought of you.
He never worshipped men of straw. Your noise
Will not disturb me, though you come again
With twice this bodyguard, *and* your commander,
So long as you are what you are.

CHORUS: Such talk
In time of trouble, sirs, cannot be well.
Just or unjust, harsh words can only harm.

MENELAUS: The archer must enjoy his little triumphs.

TEUCER: What of it? It is no craft to be ashamed of.

MENELAUS:
As a fighter fully armed there'd be no holding you.

TEUCER: What! Empty-handed I'd be a match for you
And all your armour!

MENELAUS: Hear his valiant tongue!

TEUCER: Where right is, there's excuse for boasting.

MENELAUS: Right?
What right confers a privilege on my murderer?

TEUCER: *Your* murderer? Are you risen from the dead?

MENELAUS: Thanks to a saving god. In this man's books
I was as good as dead.

TEUCER: Then pay your thanks
With honour to the gods, who let you live.

MENELAUS: When do I not pay honour to the gods?

TEUCER: When you forbid the burial of the dead.

MENELAUS: My enemy's burial – yes, I do forbid it;
  Justice forbids it.

TEUCER: Was the feud between you
  Ever declared?

MENELAUS: He hated me; I him.
  You knew it too.

TEUCER: We knew you cheated him
  By rigging votes against him.

MENELAUS: It was the court,
  Not I, that brought him down.

TEUCER: Specious excuses
  Would cover many of your shady dealings.

MENELAUS: Someone shall suffer for that insinuation!

TEUCER: We'll see that someone suffers.

MENELAUS: That is all;
  This burial is forbidden.

TEUCER: I reply,
  The burial shall go on.

MENELAUS: I've heard a man,
  A bully with his tongue, commanding sailors
  To put to sea in dirty weather; aboard
  And in the thick of the storm, you'd always find him
  Speechless, hiding his head beneath his cloak,
  And letting any man walk over him.
  That's you, and your bold language; come a gale –
  A little cloud may bring it – and your bluster
  Will soon be silenced.

TEUCER: I have seen a fool,
  Mocking his friends' misfortunes. One who stood by,
  As it might be me, feeling as I do now,
  Said to this person: 'Never insult the dead;
  You're bound to suffer for it.' So he warned
  The wretched fellow to his face. I think,
  Nay I am sure, he stands before me now,

And you are he. Is that a riddle for you?
MENELAUS: I'll go. I'd be ashamed to have it known
That I was wasting words instead of using
The power I have to force you.
TEUCER: Go then, go.
I'm bitterly ashamed of having listened
To so much windy nonsense from a fool.

Exit MENELAUS.

CHORUS: There's a mighty quarrel to come.
Make haste, sir, to find a resting-place
To keep in the memory of men
These last remains.

Enter TECMESSA *and the child.*

TEUCER: Here come his wife and son, just in fit time
To take their part in the sad ceremony ...
  Come here, my boy. Stand at your father's side,
And lay your hand upon him. He was your father.
You are his suppliant.   Now kneel, as if in prayer.
Here is my hair, and hers, and yours ... Hold them;
These are the suppliant's precious offerings.
If any man should offer violence
To move you from this dead man's side – ay, any
That bears arms here with us – so may he die
An evildoer's evil death, cut off,
Cast out unburied, his tree of life uprooted,
As I this hair do sever ... Take it, boy,
And hold it; kneel and cling to him; let none
Remove you from this place. You others, stand
Like men, not weeping women, at his side,
And keep him safe. I shall come back again,
When I have seen, in spite of all of them,
A grave made ready to receive my brother.

He goes.

CHORUS:

Will ever the days of our long sea-faring,
  Ever the tale of our toiling cease,
On Troy's wide acres warring, daring
  Danger, sharing
The shame and agony of Greece?

Would Heaven or Hell had snatched to a living
  Death that man who leagued for war
Our brother-lands, with all his striving
  Strife contriving
And death for men for evermore.

From the wine of delight and the gay flute's measure,
  From cups and garlands and blissful rest
In the arms of night, from love's dear treasure –
  From every pleasure
Brutally banished at his behest

Here we must lie on our stiff beds aching,
  Friends forgotten and far away,
Damp dews from our sodden pillows shaking,
  From cold night waking
To well-remembered Trojan day.

From the fear in the night and the flying arrow
  Ajax could shelter us; today
Grim fate has claimed his life; tomorrow
  What but sorrow
And bitterness lies in our way?

For home, for home my heart is yearning –
  To see where Sunium looks down
From her tree-topped brow on the white seas churning,
  And, homeward turning,
To greet Athena's holy crown.

After a short interval of silence, TEUCER *returns,*
followed by AGAMEMNON.

TEUCER: On guard there! Our commander, Agamemnon,
Is bearing down on us; and if I'm not mistaken,
He means to unleash the fury of his tongue
Upon our ears. I saw him and hurried back.

AGAMEMNON: Is it you, sir, bawling blasphemies against us,
As I am told, and not yet smarting for it?
And you a captive woman's brat! Great heavens,
Had you been nobly born, what huge conceit,
What strutting arrogance we should have seen,
If, being nobody, you've made yourself
The champion of this nobody. You claim,
So I have heard, that we, my brother and I,
Are not the rightful leaders of the Greeks
On land or sea, you owe us no allegiance,
And Ajax put to sea at no man's orders.
Who ever heard such impudence from underlings?
Who is this man for whom you dare to make
So loud a noise? Has he been anywhere,
Fought anywhere, where I have not? Are men
So scarce among the Greeks? That arbitration
We held about the armour of Achilles
Will cost us dear, it seems, if we're to face
At every turn the insults of a Teucer
Denouncing us as thieves, and, not content
To accept defeat and the clear verdict given
By vote of the majority, you assail us
With open threats or stab us in the back,
Because your luck was out. Heavens! at this rate
There'd be no setting up of law at all,
Were we to push aside the lawful winners
And bring the hindmost to the front. No, sir;
We'll have no more of that. Put not your trust

In broad and burly shoulders; victory
Sides with the wisest heads in every battle.
Your big-boned ox needs but a little whip
To keep him on the road; some of that medicine,
From what I see, will soon be coming your way,
Unless you get some sense into your head
And curb that insolent tongue which wags so freely
About a man that's dead and done with. Come,
Behave yourself; remember what you are,
And if you have a cause to plead before us,
Bring someone else, a free man, for your advocate.
I cannot listen to you; your barbarous speech
Sounds like a foreign language in my ears.

CHORUS: The best advice that I can offer is
That you should both become more reasonable.

TEUCER:
Who would have thought the memory of the dead
Could be so quickly blotted out, and gratitude
So soon turn traitor? Ajax, here is the man
For whom you fought, for whom you risked your life
At the spear's point over and over again, and now
He has no single word, no syllable
Of tribute to your memory. All forgotten,
All thrown aside.

(*To* AGAMEMNON)
Yes, when you spoke so wildly,
So thoughtlessly, did you remember nothing,
No day when you were penned within your fences,
Routed in battle, given up for dead,
And he came single-handed to deliver you –
No day when fire was raging round your ships,
The stern-decks all ablaze, and Hector came
Leaping over the trench to assail your fleet?
And who averted that disaster? Who

But he, who never, as you say, was seen
Where you were not? Did he not serve you well
That day? Or when he answered Hector's challenge
To single combat, under no man's orders,
Picked by the ballot; for the lot he cast
Was not of laggard clay, but light and quick
To jump to the helmet's mouth. This was the man
That did these things, and I was at his side,
Yes, I, the slave-son of a foreign mother!

    Deluded man, how can you dare to speak
So bitterly? Who was your father's father?
Was he not Pelops, a barbarian ancestor,
A Phrygian? Was not Atreus, your own father,
The perpetrator of that heinous act
The serving of his nephew's flesh for meat
Upon their father's table? You yourself
Came of a Cretan mother, and her own father
Condemned her, for adultery, to be thrown
To feed the silent fishes. Such was your origin,
And can you mock at me for what I am?
I am the son of Telamon, the man
Who won my mother as a prize for valour
And made her his; and she was royally born,
The daughter of Laomedon; my father
Had her from Hercules, Alcmena's son,
A gift of special honour. Thus nobly born
From two such noble parents, should I blush
To stand beside another of my blood,
Here so unhappily fallen, whose burial
You would forbid and do not blush to say it?
I tell you, if you cast this corpse away,
Here are three others ready to be thrown
To lie beside it; better for me to die
In his defence, here, where all men may know it,

Than fighting for your wife – or brother's wife.
Take care – for yourself, not me – for if you touch me,
You'll wish you'd been less valiant than to tempt me
With this bold challenge.

Enter ODYSSEUS.

CHORUS: Odysseus, you have come
In the nick of time, if you have come to untie
This tanglement, not make it worse confusion.

ODYSSEUS:
What's this, my friends? I heard from quite a distance
High voices raised, Agamemnon and Menelaus
Wrangling over the body of this good man.

AGAMEMNON:
And well you might; if you but knew the insults
This fellow has offered us –

ODYSSEUS: Insults? What were they?
I'd pardon a man who gave as good as he got
In wordy combat.

AGAMEMNON: I did not mince my words;
They matched the wrong that he had done me first.

ODYSSEUS: What wrong can he have done you?

AGAMEMNON: He refuses
To deny this body rites of burial
But will inter it in defiance of me.

ODYSSEUS: Will you allow a friend to speak his mind
Sincerely, and still pull his oar with you?

AGAMEMNON: I'd be a fool else. I've no better friend
Among the Greeks than you. Say what you wish.

ODYSSEUS:
It's this. For the love of all the gods, think twice
Before you do so rash and vile a thing.
You cannot leave this man to rot unburied.
You must not let your violent will persuade you
Into such hatred as would tread down justice.

There was a time when I too hated him;
From the time I won the armour of Achilles,
He was the bitterest enemy I had; and yet,
Such though he was, I could not bring myself
To grudge him honour, or refuse to admit
He was the bravest man I ever saw,
The best of all that ever came to Troy,
Save only Achilles. It is against all justice
For you to treat him with contempt. God's laws,
And not the man himself, you would annihilate.
Even if you hate him, it is against all justice
To lift your hand against a good man dead.

AGAMEMNON: Do *you*, Odysseus, take his part against me?

ODYSSEUS: I do. Yet, when there was a time to hate,
I hated him.

AGAMEMNON: Good reason to tread on him
Now he is dead!

ODYSSEUS: Such impious triumph
Should be no glory to the son of Atreus.

AGAMEMNON: What has a king to do with piety?

ODYSSEUS: At least he can respect a friend's good counsel.

AGAMEMNON: A loyal friend should listen to his superior.

ODYSSEUS: Yet consider: here you have the chance to rule
By choosing to be overruled.

AGAMEMNON: Strong pleading
In such a worthless cause.

ODYSSEUS: He was my enemy,
But he was noble.

AGAMEMNON: Are you mad? Your enemy,
And dead, and you revere him?

ODYSSEUS: Yes; his goodness
Outweighs his enmity by far.

AGAMEMNON: There speaks
A man of fickle moods.

ODYSSEUS: A friend today
  May be a foe tomorrow –

AGAMEMNON: And would you choose
  To have that kind of friend?

ODYSSEUS: I wouldn't choose
  Obstinate intolerance.

AGAMEMNON: You'd rather see me
  Branded a coward from this day on?

ODYSSEUS: No, brave
  And just, in the sight of all the Greeks.

AGAMEMNON: You say then
  I must permit the burial of this body?

ODYSSEUS: I do. Some day I too shall need that office.

AGAMEMNON:
  Ay, there you have it: every man for himself.

ODYSSEUS: Whom should I serve if not myself?

AGAMEMNON: So be it.
  Call it your act, not mine.

ODYSSEUS: Whichever you will;
  You lose no credit for it.

AGAMEMNON: I tell you this:
  For you I would do more, much more; but he,
  On earth or under it, shall be for ever
  My hated enemy. Do what you will.
                        Exit.

CHORUS: Odysseus, none but a fool would now deny
  That you have shown yourself to be a man
  Whom nature has endowed with wisdom.

ODYSSEUS: Teucer,
  I have this to say to you: I am your friend
  Henceforth, as truly as I was your enemy;
  And I am ready to help you bury your dead
  And share in every office that we mortals
  Owe to the noblest of our kind.

TEUCER: Good friend,
  I thank you for those words. You have proved me wrong
  You were my brother's bitterest enemy,
  Yet here you have stood alone in his defence,
  Refusing to be a party to gross outrage
  Offered by the living to the dead – the outrage
  Of our infatuated leader and his brother
  Who would have cast the body out with ignominy
  To rot unburied.
  So may the Father of all,
  Who rules in heaven above us, and the Avenger
  Who remembers all, and Justice, by whose hand
  The end is achieved, bring to those wicked men
  A doom as evil as that which they devised
  For this man when they wished to cast him out
  In undeserved contempt.
  But pardon me,
  Good son of Laertes, if in this burial
  I scruple to accept your helping hand,
  Which might displease the dead; but be with us
  While we perform the rites; or if you would bring
  A fellow-warrior, he will be welcome too.
  I will attend to all that must be done.
  You have been good to us.
ODYSSEUS: I would have helped you
  Gladly; but if you wish me not to do so,
  It shall be as you wish, and I will go.
                                    Exit.
TEUCER: Let us make an end. It is late.
  You, dig the deep grave quickly;
  You, the cauldron high upon the fire
  Make ready for the cleansing rites.
  The rest, bring from the tent
  His body-armour.

Come, boy, you
Are strong enough to help me lift
Your father's body.
Touch him with gentle hands.
The blood in the warm arteries
Still wells up dark and strong.
Come near, come quickly;
Here is a task
For every one that owns he is a friend
To this most perfect man.

CHORUS: Many are the things that man
Seeing must understand.
Not seeing, how shall he know
What lies in the hand
Of time to come?

EXEUNT

ELECTRA

Agamemnon and Menelaus, the sons of Atreus, held joint command of the Greek fleet and army which went to Troy to recapture Menelaus' erring wife, Helen, and wreak vengeance on the city to which she had been enticed. Before the expedition could sail from Aulis, Agamemnon was faced with the necessity to sacrifice his daughter Iphigeneia in order to propitiate Artemis and obtain a fair wind for his passage. He did this; his fleet reached Troy, and ten years later he returned victorious. But meanwhile his wife Clytaemnestra had taken Aegisthus as her lover, and together they planned to kill Agamemnon on his return. The deed was done, and Aegisthus reigned in Agamemnon's place. The daughters Electra and Chrysothemis lived on in the house of death for many years. But the youngest child, Orestes, had been entrusted by Electra to the care of a faithful friend who took him away and watched over him till he came to manhood, when he was bidden by Apollo to return home and avenge his father's death.

The play tells how he came, at first unrecognized by Electra, and then, revealing himself to her, accomplished with her help the death of their father's murderers.

ELECTRA

*

*

The scene is before the house of Agamemnon, now the house of Aegisthus, at Mycenae, overlooking the plain and city of Argos.

Enter the TUTOR, *with* ORESTES *and* PYLADES.

TUTOR: Now, son of Agamemnon, son of the great captain of the Greeks at Troy, here is a sight for you to feast your eyes on, one you have been looking forward to for many a long year. See, there is the city of your dreams, old Argos; and all the ground sacred to Inachus' daughter, Io, whom the gadfly tormented, as the story goes. Yonder is the market-place, the Lycean they call it, from the god who killed the wolf; to the left, the famous temple of Hera.

We are at Mycenae, the treasure-house of gold; and this - this is the ancestral home of the family of Pelops, a house of death if ever there was one. It was from this house I carried you away, at your sister's orders, on the day your father was murdered, all those years ago. I took you away, and looked after you, and brought you up to manhood, so that you might live to avenge your father's death.

Now, my good lads, Orestes and our friend Pylades, we must make our plans and lose no time. The starry curtain of night is drawn away, and the sun is up to wake the morning-song of birds. Let us say what we have to say before anyone comes out of doors. This is the time for action; there is no drawing back now.

ORESTES: Faithful old friend, your goodness to me is beyond question. Trust a thoroughbred horse, however old, to be keen in the charge and never fail you in a tight place; like you, carrying us forward and backing us up like the best.

Listen, and I'll tell you what I have decided, and if I'm off the mark, correct me. When I went to learn from the Pythian oracle how I was to punish my father's murderers, the reply was that I was to go alone without men or arms to help me, and by stratagem exact the just penalty of death. That was the divine command. Our plan, then, must be for you to take an opportunity of entering the house; find out what's going on inside, and bring us word. You won't be recognized after all these years. No one will know you with that white hair of yours. Spin a tale that you're a visitor from Phocis, sent by Pantheus – he's a great ally of theirs. Tell them that Orestes is dead – take your oath on it – some accidental death, say; a fall from his chariot at the Pythian games, or some such story. Meanwhile, Pylades and I will go and visit my father's grave – for the god ordered this – with libations and a lock of hair; then we'll come back, with that vessel of beaten bronze that we have hidden in the wood, and deceive them with the comfortable assurance that my body has been burned to ashes and is no more.

An ill-omened action? No matter, if a pretended death will bring me true life and glory. I call no omen bad that leads to advantage in the end. I have heard stories of sages who have been reputed dead and then have come home again to be held in new and greater honour. So I am confident that from this forged death I shall rise again like a new star to dazzle my enemies.

> May the land of our fathers, and the gods that guard
>   the land,
> Receive me and prosper the journey that I have made:
> May the house of my fathers receive me, for whose sake
> I am sent by the gods to purify and cleanse it:
> Let me not be sent away unsatisfied;
> Give me my birthright, my possession, and my home.

No more words; we'll leave you to your task, old friend; now's the time, and time is the umpire in all human business.

ELECTRA (*within*): Alas, alas!

TUTOR: Listen; someone weeping within; some servant probably.

ORESTES: Could it be poor Electra herself? Shall we wait and listen?

TUTOR: No, no. Apollo's orders first. Best start the right way, with the libation to your father; that'll put us in the way of success in all we do.

> *They leave the stage,* ORESTES *and* PYLADES *on one*
>   *side, the* TUTOR *on the other.*
> ELECTRA *comes out of the palace.*

ELECTRA: Sweet light, clean air,
  As wide as earth!
Each night that dies with dawn
I bring my sad songs here
And tear my breast until it bleeds.
Ask my uneasy bed
How many hours
In this afflicted house
I watch, how many tears I shed

For my lost father.
In all his wars abroad
He knocked in vain
At the door of death. At home
My mother and her paramour,
Aegisthus, split his skull
With an axe, as a forester
Would split an oak.
And for that piteous death,
Father, there is no mouth
But mine to cry.

My bitter tears
Shall never end,
As long as I can see
This light and the winking stars.
Like the sad bird that killed her child,
Here at my father's door
I must cry out
For all the world to hear.
Hades, Persephone,
Hermes, steward of death,
Eternal Wrath and Furies,
Children of gods,
Who see all murderers
And all adulterous thieves, come soon!
Be near me, and avenge
My father's death, and bring
My brother home!
I have no strength. I cannot stand
Alone under this load
Of my affliction.

The CHORUS *of women of Mycenae now draw near
and speak to* ELECTRA.

CHORUS: Child of a mother doomed to sin, Electra,
   Weeping ever in endless sorrow a father
   Trapped in that mother's evil snare, that lured him
   Into the hand of death, long years ago now –
   So, God forgive me, may they die that did that thing.

ELECTRA: O gentle-hearted women,
   I know you come to comfort me;
   I know, believe me, I understand.
   But I must do this, I cannot change
   Or cease to mourn for my lost father.
   You are so kind and good to me,
   Leave me and let me weep,
   Please let me weep.

CHORUS: You cannot call him back from the river of Hades,
   That all must cross, with weeping and lamentation,
   With helpless sorrow and grieving beyond all reason.
   You'll sicken to death; no tears can lighten the labour
   Of trouble past; must you still cling to misery?

ELECTRA: A dull fool might forget
   A father's miserable death.
   My way is the way of the tearful bird,
   God's messenger, that cries 'Itys! Itys!'
   Abandoned to despair. I worship Niobe,
   The inconsolable, entombed in stone,
   Weeping eternally
   With tears unceasing.

CHORUS: You are not alone, dear child, in the sorrow
   Which moves you more than the others who share your
      home;
   Your nearest kin, your sister Chrysothemis,
   And Iphianassa, they are not tired of life;
   And another – who knows where
   He hides his grief? – poor lad, waiting for the happiness,
   When God shall bring him into his princely heritage

And great Mycenae welcomes her Orestes.

ELECTRA: He is the one I am waiting for
Always and always, everywhere I go.
I have no child, no man to love,
I carry my never-ending burden,
Washed in my tears; but he has forgotten
All that was done to him, all he has heard of us.
Messages come, but only disappointment
Follows. He wants to come,
I know he wants to come, but dare not.

CHORUS: Do not despair, dear. God in heaven
Is great, he sees and governs everything.
Commit your burden of hatred into his hands;
Neither forget your enemies nor cherish
Excessive anger against them.
Time is the sacred healer; the son of Agamemnon
Will not forget; he waits in the fields of Crisa.
Nor is the Lord of the River of Death forgetful.

ELECTRA: Half my life is wasted away
In hopeless waiting; all my strength is gone.
I have no husband at my side
To fight for me, I have borne no children.
I am only an alien slave, a menial
Drudge in the house that was my father's,
Dressed like a slattern in coarse and ugly garments;
And for my sustenance
A beggar's dole at a hungry table.

CHORUS: A voice cried at his coming,
A voice cried for pity
At your father's bed, when the swift
Cut of the bronze edge flashed.
Lust and deceit were the hand and brain,
They were the parents
Of this abomination,

Whether from god or man proceeding.

ELECTRA: That was the bitterest day
  I have ever known. That night,
  That hideous banquet, the two
  Hands that my father saw
  Lifted to kill him – that made my life
  Endless captivity.
  For what they did
  May the almighty God above
  Prepare fit punishment
  And turn their pomp to ashes!

CHORUS: O say no more. Remember
  The harm you do yourself –
  Do you not see? – the mischief
  Is in your own self-torture.
  Hoarder of grief, your sullen soul
  Breeds strife unending;
  Yet when the foe is stronger
  Reason forbids to fight against him.

ELECTRA: I am beside myself,
  I know. Terrors too strong
  Have driven me down. And now
  This passion can have no end
  Till my life ends. What use is there
  In comfortable words?
  Leave me alone,
  Kind sisters, there is no escape
  From this. My sum of woe
  Outruns all reckoning.

CHORUS: Yet, child, I say with all goodwill
  And motherly love, you must not make
  Evil more evil still.

ELECTRA: How should my misery not be endless? How
  Could it ever be better to forget the dead?

Nature forbids it. That's no law for me.
Nor could I rest,
Unfaithful to my father,
In the lap of luxury, and be content
To cage the wings of lamentation.
For if the unhappy dead
Are nothing but the dust in which they lie,
And blood not paid for blood,
There is no faith, no piety, in any man.

CHORUS: Listen, my dear; it was for your good I came,
　As much as for my own; but if I cannot help you,
　Have your own way; we shall always be here if you want
　　us.

ELECTRA: I am sorry to seem so impatient, to be always
　　complaining.
　Forgive me; what else can I do? Would it not belie
　My birth and breeding to see the things I have seen
　Happening in my father's house, and not complain?
　Day in, day out, an endless summer of sorrow –
　Hating and hated by my mother – beholden to them
　For everything I may or may not do. Imagine,
　Imagine what it means to see, day after day,
　Aegisthus sitting in my father's chair, wearing
　The clothes he wore, pouring the same libations
　At the altar where he killed him: and, last outrage,
　The murderer going to his bed with *her* –
　Must I still call her mother? – with his mistress.
　For she still lives with the criminal, unashamed,
　Unafraid of retribution; on the contrary, proud
　Of the thing she did, she marks the happy day,
　The day she treacherously killed my father,
　With music and sacrifice, as each month comes round,
　To thank the saving gods. And I must watch
　And weep alone at the foul ceremonies

That keep his name alive – but weep in silence,
Not as my heart would have me weep. This woman,
This queen of falsehood, scolds me: 'What!' she says,
'Are you the first to lose a father, then?
Is no one else in mourning? Worthless slut,
Death take you! And I pray the infernal gods
Will never deliver you from your misery!' –
Nagging like that; except when there is rumour
Of Orestes' coming; then she loses her temper
And raves to my face. 'This is your doing,' she says.
'It's you I have to thank for this. You stole him
Out of my arms and had him sent away.
You'll get what you deserve, make no mistake.'
Her voice rises to a scream, and her noble lord
Stands by and takes her part – a skulking villain,
A coward hiding behind a woman's skirts.
So I can do nothing but wait in my misery
For Orestes to come and put an end to it.
He always meant to do it, and I have waited
And waited till all the hope I ever had
Is worn away. How can you tell me to be calm
And dutiful? With evil all around me
There is nothing I can do that is not evil.

CHORUS:
Do you mean – is Aegisthus here at the present moment,
Or away from home?

ELECTRA: He is away just now.
You may be sure I should not venture out
If he were near. He is out of the town today.

CHORUS: If that is so, may I speak freely to you?

ELECTRA: Yes, while he is away. What is it you want?

CHORUS:
We want to know about your brother. What news?
Is he coming or not? We do so want to know.

ELECTRA: He promises – but his promises come to nothing.
CHORUS: A man may well be chary of such a task.
ELECTRA: Was I chary of saving his life?
CHORUS: Take heart.
   He's a good man, and will stand by his kith and kin.
ELECTRA: I trust so; else I could not have lived so long.
CHORUS: Say no more now. Here is your sister,
   Chrysothemis, coming from the house with the oblations
   Due to be made to those that lie below.

> CHRYSOTHEMIS *comes from the palace carrying*
> *sepulchral offerings.*

CHRYSOTHEMIS:
   Electra! Why are you here again, out of doors,
   And holding forth in this fashion? Have you not learnt
   After all this time to restrain your useless anger,
   Not make a vain parade of it? I'm sure
   I feel our position as bitterly as you do,
   And if only I had the strength to do it, I'd show
   Where my real feelings lie. But as it is,
   My policy is to bow before the storm,
   Not make a show of pluck, when powerless
   To strike a blow. I wish you'd do the same.
   O yes, it's true that what you think is right,
   Not what I say. And yet, to keep my freedom,
   I know I must obey.

ELECTRA:
   You ought to be ashamed, if you're our father's daughter,
   To forget him and to take your mother's part.
   The lessons you read to me are not your own,
   She taught you them. You cannot have it both ways;
   Either defy her, or forget your friends
   And be an obedient daughter. You said just now
   That if you had the strength you'd show us all
   How much you hate those two; yet here am I

Trying to help my father all I can
And you do nothing but thwart me. Must we be cowards.
As well as slaves? Why, tell me if you can
How would it help me to renounce this sorrow?
I have my life – bare life, but it is enough
As long as I can still torment my jailers
To gratify the dead – if any joy
Can touch the dead. Your way of showing resentment
Is only words; in deeds you're on their side,
Your father's murderers' accomplice. Never
Would I give in to them – no, not for all
The privileges on which you pride yourself,
Your luxuries and your comforts; you can keep them.
I have my peace of mind; that is enough
For me to live on. I don't want your position;
Neither would you, if you were not deluded.
Instead of daughter to the noblest father
That ever lived, call yourself mother's daughter,
Then everyone will know you for what you are,
Disloyal to your dead father and your friends.

CHORUS: For the gods' sake, do not quarrel. There is some-
        thing to be said
   On either side, and each might learn a lesson
   From the other.

CHRYSOTHEMIS: I know her arguments by heart!
   I wouldn't have brought the matter up at all,
   Had I not heard of the terrible punishment
   In store for her, to end her long complaining.

ELECTRA:
   What punishment? Tell me of anything worse than this
   That I suffer now, and I will say no more.

CHRYSOTHEMIS: I will; I'll tell you everything I know.
   If you will not cease from wailing, you are to be sent
   To some place where you'll never see the light

For ever more, banished, to end your life
Singing sad dirges in a vaulted dungeon.
Think over that, and when the sentence falls,
Don't tell me I was wrong. Be wiser now
While there is time.

ELECTRA: Is this decided, then?

CHRYSOTHEMIS:
And when Aegisthus comes, it will be done.

ELECTRA: If that is all, the sooner he comes the better.

CHRYSOTHEMIS: Fool, what do you mean?

ELECTRA: If it is as you say,
Let him come quickly.

CHRYSOTHEMIS: Are you out of your mind?
Can you want to suffer so?

ELECTRA: Yes, to escape
Far, far out of the sight of all of you.

CHRYSOTHEMIS:
With no regret for life as you know it now?

ELECTRA: Life as I know it! How marvellously fair!

CHRYSOTHEMIS: It could be, if you chose to make it so.

ELECTRA: You mean if I betrayed my best-beloved?

CHRYSOTHEMIS:
Nothing of the sort; only obey your masters.

ELECTRA: And cringe, as you do? I couldn't find it in me.

CHRYSOTHEMIS:
No one would wish you to fall by your own folly.

ELECTRA: I will fall, if need be, for my father's sake.

CHRYSOTHEMIS: But I believe our father will pardon us.

ELECTRA: Cowards believe such comfortable things.

CHRYSOTHEMIS: Well, you won't listen to my advice.

ELECTRA: I won't.
I'll never be so foolish.

CHRYSOTHEMIS: Then I'll go.

ELECTRA: Where are you going? What offerings are those?

CHRYSOTHEMIS:
  Our mother's libations for our father's grave.
ELECTRA: Libations! For the man she ... hated most?
CHRYSOTHEMIS:
  The man she killed – is what you meant to say.
ELECTRA: By whose advice? Who wanted her to do it?
CHRYSOTHEMIS:
  I think she has had some frightening dream.
ELECTRA (*her face lighting up with hope*): O gods,
  Gods of our fathers, now be with us at last!
CHRYSOTHEMIS:
  Why, does her fear give you some ground for hope?
ELECTRA: I cannot tell as yet. What has she seen?
CHRYSOTHEMIS: I only know a little –
ELECTRA: What do you know?
  Fate often hangs upon a word or two.
CHRYSOTHEMIS:
  I was told she saw our father returned to life,
  Standing beside her; and he took the sceptre
  That once was his, which now Aegisthus carries,
  And planted it near the altar, where it sprouted
  Into a leafy bough, casting a shadow
  Over all Mycenae. This much I was told
  By someone who heard her telling the Sun her dream.
  That is all I know; but I know it was that vision
  That made her send me here. Now will you listen
  To my advice? By all the gods, I beg you
  To save yourself from perishing in your folly.
  Refuse, and you'll be coming to me for help
  When worse befalls.
ELECTRA (*in a more friendly mood*): Listen to me, my dear.
  None of those things you have must touch the tomb.
  You have no warrant in justice or in piety
  For bringing libations or offerings to our father

From the wife who hated him. Throw them away;
Bury them deep in the ground, far from the place
Where our father sleeps. She'll find them when she dies
Reserved to grace her own black burial!
Only the hardest woman that ever lived
Could bring herself to offer such grim gifts
To the man she killed. How can you think the dead
Could gratefully take such tributes from the fiend
That mercilessly killed and butchered him
And wiped her bloody sword upon his hair?
Will these gifts clean her hands? Never on earth.
Throw them away.
This is what you must give him . . .
A lock of your own bright hair . . . and this of mine –
In my poor state it is all I have to give –
There . . . it's not glossy like yours . . . This girdle too,
It's only plain, but take it. Kneel to him
And pray that he himself will come from the dead
To befriend us and help us against our enemies;
And that Orestes may be alive and coming in strength
To crush his father's enemies under his foot;
So that when next we come to deck his grave
We may have richer ornaments than these to give him.
For truly I think it was in part his doing
That she was visited by that frightening dream.
Be that as it may; go, sister, and do this service
To help us both, and him that lies below,
The dearest and best of fathers.

CHORUS: O dear lady,
Your sister speaks from the devotion of her heart.
You would be wise to do what she has asked.

CHRYSOTHEMIS: I will.
Duty is not a thing to be argued about,
But to be done, the sooner the better. But O my friends,

If I do this, help me, for the love of heaven,
By your silence. If my mother hears of it,
I may have cause to be sorry for my presumption.

She goes.

CHORUS:
This omen, if I rightly understand
Its message, and am not deceived,
Speaks with the voice of Justice, and ere long
She will be here and fighting for us
In all her righteous strength.
That dream we heard of
Breathes comfort and new courage.
Your royal father has not forgotten you,
Nor does the bronze blade sleep.
The two-edged axe that struck the impious blow
So long ago, remembers.
The Avenger lies in wait; the feet, the hands
Are closing in, the bronze hoof stamps.
When lust and murder and mockery of marriage
Have desecrated the bed, defied the law,
What can such portents mean
If not the downfall
Of culprits and confederates?
Men may well despair of interpreting
Dreams and the signs of heaven
If this night's vision does not point the way
To a safe and happy issue.

See what a heavy load of enduring sorrow
For all our land
Was borne on Pelops' chariot-wheels!
Thrown from his golden car
By a wicked trick,
Myrtilus went to his death

And the sea closed over him,
And from that day
This house has never seen the end
Of shame and misery.

Enter CLYTAEMNESTRA *from the palace.*

CLYTAEMNESTRA: So here you are, Electra. Wandering at
your own sweet will, now that Aegisthus is away. He could
at least keep you from straying out of bounds, and dis-
gracing your family before the world. You take no notice
of me, it seems, when he is not here; and yet you spread it
about that I am a cruel and unjust tyrant who treats you and
all you love with insult. I do not insult anybody; if I speak
harshly to you, it is only because I get nothing but harsh
words from you. You say it is because I caused your father's
death. It is true. I don't forget it; and I have no wish to
deny it, since it was not my doing alone; I had an ally –
Justice. And you should have been on the side of Justice too,
if you knew where your duty lay.

This father of yours, whom you never stop weeping for,
did a thing no other Greek had dared to do, when he so
ruthlessly sacrificed your sister to the gods – the child whom
he had begotten, at little cost of course compared to mine
who bore her. No doubt you can tell me why he did this,
and for whose sake? For the Greeks, maybe? And who gave
them the right to take my daughter's life? ... Or for
Menelaus? Is that any reason why he should not be brought
to justice for killing what was mine? Had not Menelaus two
children of his own? And should not they have been the
ones to die, the children of that father, that mother, the cause
of the whole enterprise? Was my child's blood sweeter to
the stomach of Death than Helen's? Or had that monstrous
father transferred to Menelaus' children all the love he had
ceased to feel for mine?

If you think such a thing could be the action of a sane and
prudent parent, I do not. And she that is dead would say the
same, if she could. No, I've nothing to regret. You think
I'm heartless. You would do well to make sure of your own
ground before condemning others.

ELECTRA: I'm sure I have given you no provocation this
time for speaking as you do. But with your leave, I would
like to say what I think may be justly said for my dead father
and for my sister.

CLYTAEMNESTRA: Certainly you may. If you always began
in that tone, it would be a pleasure to listen to you.

ELECTRA: This is my case. You admit you killed my father;
And that is the most monstrous admission you could make,
Whether you had justice on your side or not.
I say you had not; you were drawn on and cajoled
By the wiles of the miscreant whom you are living with now.
Ask Huntress Artemis what fault she punished
By withholding the winds that blow on the straits of Aulis.
I'll tell you, since we cannot question her.

I have heard how my father, in an idle moment,
Walking in a demesne of the goddess, startled a stag,
A dappled full-antlered beast, and thoughtlessly
With a rash triumphant cry he shot it dead.
It was this that provoked the goddess, Leto's daughter,
To detain the Greeks and make my father pay
For the creature's life by offering up his daughter.
So she was sacrificed; there was no other way
To get the ships afloat, either for Troy
Or homeward. This was the reason why he was forced
Against his will, and after much resistance,
To make the sacrifice. It was not done
To humour Menelaus. Even if it were,
As you maintain, even if that were his object,
To help his brother, would that entitle you

To take his life? What kind of law is that?
Lay down *that* law, and you will bind yourself
To bitter regret. If life for life be the rule,
Justice demands *your* life before all others.
The excuse you plead is no excuse; explain,
If you please, what justification you have
For your present abominable way of life –
Mistress of the murderer that helped you kill my father,
Bearing his children to supplant the innocent
Legitimate offspring whom you have driven away.
Is there any excuse for this? Vengeance perhaps
For your stolen daughter's life? If that is your plea,
It does you little credit; there's little to boast of
In trying to make your daughter an excuse
For such an impious marriage.

    But I must not lecture you; you only retort
Time and again, that I am insolent to my mother –
Mother! – more like a jailer, with the slavery
You put upon me, the insults I have to bear
From you and your partner ...
And somewhere far away
Is another who barely escaped your clutches – Orestes,
In long unhappy exile. I kept him alive,
You have often said, to be your executioner.
Yes, if I could, I would have done just that,
I tell you to your face. Denounce me for it,
Denounce me in public, call me what you will –
Vile, brutal, shameless – if I am all these,
I am your true daughter!

CHORUS: She is angry now,
    And little concerned with justice, if you ask me.

CLYTAEMNESTRA:
    I've reason to be concerned with her, I think,
    If this is the language she uses to her mother –

And she a grown woman. Is there anything
She will not stoop to? She has no shame at all.

ELECTRA: I *am* ashamed, believe me, for what I have said;
You may not think it, but I am ashamed
Of my rudeness and ill-temper. It is you,
Your hatred and ill-treatment, drive me on
To act against my nature; villainy
Is taught by vile example.

CLYTAEMNESTRA: Impudent creature!
You talk a deal too much of what I do
And what I say!

ELECTRA: Not I. Your every action
Speaks for itself.

CLYTAEMNESTRA: Now by the blessed Artemis,
You shall be punished, when Aegisthus comes!

ELECTRA: So you are angry now; you gave me leave
To speak my mind, and still you will not listen.

CLYTAEMNESTRA:
I have let you speak; now will you hold your tongue
And let me make my vows?

ELECTRA: Make them; my voice
Shall trouble you no longer.

CLYTAEMNESTRA (*to her attendant*): Lift up the fruit-offer-
ing, that I may pray to the Lord of this altar for ease
from my present fears.
Phoebus, our Guardian, hear my prayer,
Though spoken under concealment,
Not openly as among friends. There stands one near me,
Before whom I dare not freely unveil my thoughts
To let her busy and malicious tongue
Plant seed of scandal in every street.
I speak as I must; hear Thou as I would be heard.
O Lord Lycean,
If it was for my good,

That dream of double-meaning that I saw this night,
Let its fulfilment come; but if for ill,
Then let it fall on those that wish me ill.
If there be any plotting in secret
Against my present welfare, hinder them;
And grant that I may long live safe from harm,
Queen of this house and country,
Living in happiness with those who love me,
As I live now,
With all my children who bear no malice
Or bitter hate against me.
Lycean Apollo, graciously hear me,
And grant to us all our desires.
The rest Thou surely knowest, though I be silent,
For Thou art a god.
And do not the sons of God see all?

Enter the TUTOR.

TUTOR: Kind ladies, am I right in thinking this is the house of King Aegisthus?

CHORUS: You are quite right, sir; it is.

TUTOR: And this lady, I think, is his wife, is she not? There is royalty in her looks.

CHORUS: Right again. It is she that stands before you.

TUTOR (*to* CLYTAEMNESTRA): Greetings to your Majesty. I am the bearer of glad news from a friend, to you and to your lord Aegisthus.

CLYTAEMNESTRA: A welcome omen indeed. Tell me first, whose messenger you are.

TUTOR: The messenger of Phanoteus of Phocis, and the message one that concerns you deeply.

CLYTAEMNESTRA: Tell it me. You come from a friend, so I have no fear that your message will be anything but friendly.

TUTOR: Orestes is dead; that is all.

ELECTRA: O no! I cannot bear it!

CLYTAEMNESTRA: What, what, sir? Never mind her.

TUTOR: As I said, Orestes has died.

ELECTRA: O, this is the end, the end of everything for me!

CLYTAEMNESTRA: Mind your own business, you. Tell me, sir, tell me everything; how did he die?

TUTOR: I will tell you everything. It was for that purpose I was sent.

Orestes had gone to Delphi, to compete in the games which are the prime festival of Hellas; and on the proclamation of the first event, the foot-race, he stepped forward, his brilliant figure exciting the admiration of all present. His performance matched the promise, and he returned the winner of the coveted prize. After that, well – to cut a long story short – I never saw such a triumph. In point of fact, there was not an event announced in all the foot-racing in which he did not win a prize; and how they cheered him every time his name rang out: 'Orestes of Argos, son of Agamemnon, commander-in-chief of the famous Hellenic army.'

So far, so good. But the assaults of heaven are more than the strongest man can withstand. The day for the chariot-races came, and the contest was to start at sunrise. Orestes was there, with many another competitor: an Achaean, a Spartan, two drivers of teams from Libya, and Orestes with his Thessalian horses – that makes five – an Aetolian with chestnut colts, six, a Magnesian, seven – an Aenian with a white team, and one from the sacred walls of Athens, eight, nine – and a Boeotian, ten.

The appointed stewards cast the lots for position and ranged the chariots on the starting-line; then, at the sound of the bronze trumpet, off they started, all shouting to their horses and twitching the reins in their hands. The clatter of the rattling chariots filled the whole arena, and the dust flew up as they sped along in a dense mass, each driver goading his team unmercifully in his efforts to draw clear of the rival axles and panting steeds, whose steaming breath and sweat drenched every bending back and flying wheel together.

To begin with, all went well with every chariot. Then the Aenian's tough colts took the bit in their teeth and on the turn from the sixth to the seventh lap, ran head-on into the African. This accident led to other upsets and collisions, till the field of Crisa was a sea of wrecked and capsized chariots. The Athenian driver had seen what was coming and was clever enough to draw aside and bide his time while the oncoming wave crashed into inextricable confusion. Orestes was driving last, purposely holding his team back and pinning his faith to the final spurt; and now, seeing only one rival left in, with an exultant shout to his swift horses he drove hard ahead and the two teams raced neck and neck, now one now the other gaining a lead.

At each turn of the lap, Orestes reined in his inner trace-horse and gave the outer its head, so skilfully that his hub just cleared the post by a hair's breadth every time; and so the poor fellow had safely rounded every lap but one without mishap to himself or his chariot. But at the last he misjudged the turn, slackened his left rein before the horse was safely round the bend, and so fouled the post. The hub was smashed across, and he was hurled over the rail entangled in the severed reins, and as he fell his horses ran wild across the course.

When the people saw his fall from the chariot, there was a cry of sympathy for the poor lad – the hero of such magnificent exploits and now the victim of such a terrible misfortune. They saw him now pinned to the ground, now rolled head over heels, till at last the other drivers got his runaway horses under control and extricated the poor mangled body, so bruised and bloody that not one of his friends could have recognized him. They carried him straight to a pyre and burned him; and shortly some men of Phocis will be bringing you a little urn of bronze that contains, alas, the dust of one of the greatest of men, so that you may lay him to rest in his native soil.

Such is my sad story, sad indeed to hear, but to us who witnessed it more terrible than anything I ever saw.

CHORUS: So now the last of our royal and ancient house
Is lost and the name blotted out for ever!

CLYTAEMNESTRA: O God,
Is this good news, or something that I must suffer
For my advantage? I cannot help but suffer,
When my own loss is the price of my own living.

TUTOR:
I did not think you would grieve so much at my news.

CLYTAEMNESTRA: Can a mother not grieve? Can any enmity
sever her love for the child of her own flesh?

TUTOR: I see my errand was a thankless one.

CLYTAEMNESTRA:
No, no, not that; not thankless; you have come
To bring me proof that he is dead; proof positive
That he is dead. His life was given from mine,
And from the breast that nursed him he went out
To be a stranger in exile. From that day on
He never saw my face, yet held me guilty
Of his father's death, and swore to punish me.
And here I lay, by day or night denied
The cloak of sleep; Time's prisoner, condemned
To wait for loitering death. Now I am free,
Free of all fear of him, and free of *her*,
That even greater spoiler of my peace,
That serpent sucking out my heart's red wine!

We shall have no more of her ugly warnings now,
And I can live in peace.

ELECTRA: O misery!
My poor Orestes ... to have suffered so ...
And this is your mother's tribute to your memory!
Can this be justice?

CLYTAEMNESTRA: Justice is done to him,
Not yet to you.

ELECTRA: Goddess of Vengeance, hear
And speak for the dead!

CLYTAEMNESTRA: She has heard most faithfully
And spoken well.

ELECTRA: Gloat on your triumph, gloat!

CLYTAEMNESTRA: Will you and Orestes give me leave?

ELECTRA: It is we
Who are silenced, and have no power to silence you.

CLYTAEMNESTRA (to TUTOR):
Well sir, if you could have stopped this clamorous tongue,
Your news would have been worth a mint of money.

TUTOR: I had better go, madam, if there's nothing else –

CLYTAEMNESTRA:
Go? No, you shall not go; it wouldn't be fair
To myself or to my friend who sent you here.
Come in; we'll leave her here, to cry her heart out
For herself and her beloved.

She takes him into the palace.

ELECTRA: There's a fine picture of a parent's grief –
The mourning of a poor heartbroken mother
For a son so lost; a sneer, and she is gone.
Orestes, my darling, you are dead, how can I live?
Your going has torn the last shred of hope from my heart,
The hope that you would come again alive
To avenge your father and save your unhappy sister.
Now where can I go? No brother; no father; alone.

There is nothing for me but to go back to my slavery
In this hateful house, my father's murderers' house.
Can this be justice? No, I will not go back,
Nor ever set foot in the house again. Here,
Here at the door I will lie and starve to death,
For I have no friend in the world.
Let them come and kill me
If they hate me so; to kill me would be kindness;
Life is all pain to me; I want to die.

She sinks to the ground.

CHORUS: Is there no Sun to light,
  No thunder in heaven, none
  To smite such infamy?

ELECTRA (*in broken sobs*): Ah, ah . . .

CHORUS: Why, dear one –

ELECTRA: Ah . . .

CHORUS: You must not cry.

ELECTRA: Do not torment me!

CHORUS: I?

ELECTRA: Can you insult my sorrow
  Speaking of hope
  When he is surely dead?

CHORUS: There was a king, beguiled
  To his death by a collar of gold,
  Yet in the grave –

ELECTRA: Ah, ah . . .

CHORUS: He lived to reign.

ELECTRA: Alas.

CHORUS: Ah, the murderess –

ELECTRA: She paid with her life?

CHORUS: True.

ELECTRA: The afflicted found a friend;
  He that was mine
  Is lost, and I have no other.

CHORUS: Your lot is hard.

ELECTRA: I know,
How well I know.
Through every month of the year
My river of life
Is a spate of sorrow.

CHORUS: We have seen your tears.

ELECTRA: Do not forbid me them.
This is the end –

CHORUS: The end?

ELECTRA: Of all the hope I had
Of the one that shared my royal blood.

CHORUS: All men must die.

ELECTRA: As he
Was doomed to die?
Dragged in a tangle of reins,
Trapped in a mêlée of flying hoofs?

CHORUS: A terrible end.

ELECTRA: And the worst: in a foreign land
Hidden away –

CHORUS: Ay, ay.

ELECTRA: Without my hands, my tears,
To send him safe to his resting-place.

Enter CHRYSOTHEMIS *in joyful excitement.*

CHRYSOTHEMIS: Electra, my dearest! O I am so happy,
I had to come in almost indecent haste
To tell you at once. Such joyful news, my dear!
This is the cure for all your woes and sorrows.

ELECTRA: What cure can there be for my incurable wounds?

CHRYSOTHEMIS: Orestes is here; truly, beyond a doubt
He is here, as sure as I stand before you now.

ELECTRA:
Are you mad, woman? Or making fun of the misery
That you and I both suffer?

CHRYSOTHEMIS: No, I swear
  By our hearth and home, I am not making fun.
  He is here, I tell you; he has come back to us.
ELECTRA: Alas, no. What makes you believe that story?
  From whom did you hear it?
CHRYSOTHEMIS: I didn't hear it from anyone;
  I believe the evidence which I saw with my own eyes.
ELECTRA:
  What evidence can you have seen? What light of mischief
  Is this that is kindled in you? What have you seen?
CHRYSOTHEMIS:
  Listen, for God's sake, to what I have to tell you,
  Then tell me whether I am mad or not.
ELECTRA: Tell me, if you must.
CHRYSOTHEMIS: I'll tell you everything.
  I went to the ancient tomb where our father lies,
  And there, on the top of the sepulchre, I saw
  The marks of a new libation of milk, and garlands
  Of flowers of every kind encircling the grave.
  I was astonished to see them, and looked carefully round
  In case there was anyone there. But all was quiet.
  So I crept nearer to the tomb; and there at its edge
  I found a lock of hair, newly cut off.
  And O, when I saw it, at once my heart was filled
  With the thought of my best beloved, my own Orestes.
  I took it up in my hands, in reverent silence,
  But weeping for joy, knowing, as I knew at once,
  That no one else could have brought that offering.
  Who else should do such a thing but you or I?
  I know it was not I; nor you – how could you,
  When you are strictly forbidden to leave the house
  Even for worship? Nor is it the kind of thing
  Our mother likes to do, or if she did
  Could do without our knowledge.

They are surely Orestes' offerings. Courage, my dear!
No one's fortune in life is fixed for ever.
Fate has been hard on us; who knows? – this day
May be the beginning of untold happiness.

ELECTRA: O you are a fool! I can only pity you still.

CHRYSOTHEMIS:
Why, Electra, aren't you glad at what I have told you?

ELECTRA: You are in a dreamland of your own imagining.

CHRYSOTHEMIS: Dreams? Why should I dream what I have
seen in the daylight?

ELECTRA: He is dead, my dear. You must hope no longer
For help from him. Think no more of him.

CHRYSOTHEMIS: O no! It cannot be true. Who told you?

ELECTRA: Someone who was with him when he died.

CHRYSOTHEMIS: I cannot believe it. Where is he now?

ELECTRA: In the house. Mother is making him welcome.

CHRYSOTHEMIS:
How terrible! But who can have made those offerings
So generously at our father's grave?

ELECTRA: Someone, I suppose, has put them there
In memory of Orestes who is dead.

CHRYSOTHEMIS:
Then all is sadness still. And to think I came
In such haste with my joyful news, in ignorance
Of the depth of our misfortune, only to find
New and worse trouble added to the old.

ELECTRA: Yes, it is true. And now, if you will listen,
You may learn how to lighten the load of our present
sorrows.

CHRYSOTHEMIS:
Would you have me raise the dead to life again?

ELECTRA: No. That is not what I mean. I am not so foolish.

CHRYSOTHEMIS: What can I do?

ELECTRA: Be brave enough to obey me.

CHRYSOTHEMIS: I am ready to do whatever may be useful.

ELECTRA: Remember, there is no success without an effort.

CHRYSOTHEMIS: I know. I'll play my part as well as I can.

ELECTRA: This is my plan, then.

You know as well as I
We haven't a friend left; death has taken them all,
And we are alone. As long as there was any news
Of our brother alive and well, I went on hoping
For the day when he would come to settle accounts
With our father's murderers. Now that he is dead,
I turn to you; will you be brave enough
To help me kill the man who killed our father,
Aegisthus? There, the secret's out . . .
Why, woman,
What are you waiting for? What hope is there
To cling to still? A lifetime of regret
For your lost inheritance, a dismal prospect
Of ageing spinsterhood? You've little chance
Of ever being bride or wife; Aegisthus
Knows better than to let our tree bear fruit;
Life born from you or me would mean his death.
But if you listen to my advice, and follow it,
You will be doing your pious duty to the dead,
Our father and our brother, and live henceforth
A free woman, worthy of the name you bear,
With a marriage to be proud of. Courage is a thing
All men admire. Think what it will mean
For your good name and mine, if you do this;
How all our people will greet us with admiration,
And strangers too. 'Look,' they will say to their friends;
'Those two sisters upheld the honour of their house,
Stood up to an enemy in the flush of his success,
And risked their own two lives to avenge a death.
We owe them all our love and respect; such courage

Must have honourable recognition on holy days
And state occasions.' That is how they'll speak of us
All over the world, to our everlasting honour
In life or in death.
Come, my dear, say you'll do it.
Fight on your father's side, on your brother's side;
Put an end to my shame and yours; for shame it is,
No less, when noble natures are brought low.
CHORUS: This is a time when none should speak or listen
Without great caution.
CHRYSOTHEMIS: Very true, my friends.
I think my sister would have been well-advised
To use more caution before speaking thus.
(*To* ELECTRA)
I wonder, Electra, what can have possessed you
To put on such bold armour, and call on me
To serve under your orders? Do you forget
You are only a woman, and weaker than your enemy?
His day is rising, ours is running out
And almost ended. Who could set a snare
For such a man, and not himself be caught
In the net of doom? Take care; this kind of talk,
If anyone hears it, will bring us from bad to worse.
Honour and glory will do us little good
If we die an ignominious death for it.
Nor is death the worst we can look for; lingering life,
And death denied, may be still deadlier.
O Electra, for pity's sake, think what you do
Before you destroy us all and end our history
For ever. What you have said shall not go further,
I'll see to that; nothing will come of it,
It is late, but not too late, to learn the wisdom
Of bowing, when helpless, to the powers set over us.
CHORUS: Yes, yes, Electra, listen; prudence and caution

Are the only things worth having in this life.

ELECTRA (*to* CHRYSOTHEMIS):
It is just as I expected. I always knew
You would have nothing to do with my proposal.
Then I must do the thing myself, alone,
For done it must be.

CHRYSOTHEMIS: It is a thousand pities
You had not shown the same determination
The day our father died. You could have done much.

ELECTRA: The will indeed was there, but the wit was weaker.

CHRYSOTHEMIS:
Would you could keep it so as long as you live.

ELECTRA: That means you have no intention of helping me?

CHRYSOTHEMIS:
It does. The attempt is bound to end in disaster.

ELECTRA: I admire your caution; but I despise your spirit.

CHRYSOTHEMIS: I accept your insults, as I shall your thanks
When the time comes.

ELECTRA: The time will never come.

CHRYSOTHEMIS: We can but wait and see.

ELECTRA: Away with you;
You are no help to me at all.

CHRYSOTHEMIS: I could be,
If you knew how to listen.

ELECTRA: Go, then, go
And tell your mother everything you've heard.

CHRYSOTHEMIS: I do not hate you that much.

ELECTRA:
Then I hope you understand how much you hurt me.

CHRYSOTHEMIS:
Hurt you? When my only thought is how to save you?

ELECTRA: And must I walk by *your* light?

CHRYSOTHEMIS: Till your own
Is clear enough to guide us both.

ELECTRA: How clever,
  And yet how blind!

CHRYSOTHEMIS: Your malady exactly.

ELECTRA: Do you deny the justice of my case?

CHRYSOTHEMIS: Justice is sometimes dangerous.

ELECTRA: Heaven forbid
  That I should walk by such a precept.

CHRYSOTHEMIS: Well,
  If you do this thing, you'll find that I was right.

ELECTRA:
  I'll do it; your threats don't frighten me; I'll do it.

CHRYSOTHEMIS:
  Do you mean it, Electra? Won't you be advised
  To change your mind?

ELECTRA: I won't be *ill* advised;
  No good can come of that.

CHRYSOTHEMIS: You seem determined
  To disagree with me.

ELECTRA: My mind has been made up
  A long time now.

CHRYSOTHEMIS: I'll go, then; you cannot bear
  To listen to me, nor I to give consent
  To what you are doing.

ELECTRA: Go ... I cannot walk
  Your way, plead as you will. Don't chase illusions;
  That's the unwisest thing of all.

CHRYSOTHEMIS: I see.
  If you're so satisfied with your own wisdom,
  Then follow it. But when the trouble comes,
  You'll thank me for my warning.

                    Exit.

CHORUS:
  Will we not learn?
  Even the birds of the air

Know in their wisdom how to tend
With affectionate care
The parents to whom they owe their birth
And living. Can we in turn
Not pay
Our debts as well as they?
As there is Justice in heaven
And fire in the hand of God,
The reckoning must be made in the end.
Let the earth cry to the dead, cry
To the grave where the sons of Atreus lie,
Let a voice proclaim
The infamy, speak of the shame!

Discord within,
Dividing child from child,
Sisters at enmity, strife
Unreconciled
By charity in their daily lives.
For their father one alone
Must weep
Abandoned on the deep
Ocean of tears, Electra,
Like a bird that cries in the night
In unconsolable grief. For life
She cares no longer, she would fain
Die to rid her house of the tyranny
Of the coupled fiends. So rare
A pattern of breed we shall not see again.

For this is true nobility,
Never to shame
By life ingloriously bought
An honourable name.
You, child, have chosen so,

For ever to take your part
With those that suffer,
Armed against evil, and to win
The twofold crown,
Wisdom and piety.

Yet may your hand and weal
Ascend as high
Above your enemy's head
As now you lie
Beneath his feet. No joy
Was ever in your path of life;
Yet you lived faithfully
In duty to God
And to the great eternal laws, and found
In these your victory.

> ORESTES *and* PYLADES *enter from the side of the stage.*
> PYLADES *is carrying a small funeral urn.*

ORESTES: If you please, good ladies, we are not sure if we are on the right road, or if we have misunderstood our directions.

CHORUS: Where are you bound for, sir, and what is your business?

ORESTES: I am trying to find the place where Aegisthus lives.

CHORUS: Then you have found it; your informant was quite correct.

ORESTES: Which of you, I wonder, would be so good as to tell them within that a long expected visitor is here?

CHORUS: That should be the privilege of the nearest of kin; and here she is.

ORESTES (*to* ELECTRA): Please say that some gentlemen of Phocis are asking for Aegisthus.

ELECTRA: O the sad day! – Is this the confirmation of the news that we have just heard?

ORESTES: I don't know what news that was, lady. My
　　message is from our elder Strophius and concerns Orestes.
ELECTRA: Tell it me, sir. – I am afraid to hear it.
ORESTES: As you see, we have brought this little urn which
　　contains the little that is left of him – for he is dead.
ELECTRA: Yes, I see ... you have it there in your hands ...
　　there is no doubt, then ... O my brother!
ORESTES: You weep, lady, I know, for what has happened
　　to Orestes. It is in truth his dust that lies here.
ELECTRA: His dust lies there ... Please give it to me, sir.
　　I want to hold it in my hands, and weep,
　　Weep over this dust, and remember with tears
　　All my sorrow and the sorrow of all my house.
ORESTES: Who is she? (*To* PYLADES) Bring it to her and
　　let her hold it.
　　She cannot have any ill purpose in asking for it.
　　No doubt she is a friend, or one of his family.
　　　　The urn is given into ELECTRA's *hands.*

ELECTRA: So here is all that is left of my beloved,
　　Orestes; only this to remember you by,
　　My dearest on earth. Did I think to welcome you back
　　Thus, when last I parted from you – thus,
　　A handful of nothing? Is this the lovely child
　　I said goodbye to? It would have been much better
　　If I had died instead of trying to save you
　　By smuggling you away to another land
　　To keep you alive; you could have died that day
　　And shared your father's grave – instead of this,
　　This cruel death in exile, far from home,
　　Far from your sister. And I could not be there
　　To wash and dress your body for the fire
　　Or dutifully lift the sad remains
　　In loving hands. All this was left for strangers

To do for you, my dearest, till you came
Home to us here, this little pot of dust.
  I used to nurse you in the days gone by;
Is this the end of all that loving labour?
You were more my child than mother's; no one else
Looked after you but I; 'sister' you called me,
As if you had no other. Now you are dead,
And all is ended in a day; all gone
Like dust upon the wind, now you are gone.
Our father is dead; and what am I but dead
Since you have died and gone away without me?
The fiends are laughing now; that mother-monster
Runs mad with joy; you used to send me messages,
Do you remember, secretly, about her
And how you'd soon be here to punish her.
But that's all ended, thanks to the evil demon
That fights against you and me, the same that took
My lovely brother from me and sent home
Dust and a shadow.
O my own,
My poor dear darling,
Death lay in the way you had to walk, and I
Must die, must die with your death. O my brother,
Let me come home with you, dead with the dead,
To stay with you for ever. While you were here,
We shared and shared alike; now let me die
And be where you are, where all sorrow ends
For ever.
CHORUS: Electra, think, your father had to die,
  Orestes had to die; this is a thing
  We all must suffer; do not weep too much.
ORESTES: What can I say?
  God help me, what can I say?
  Silence will stifle me.

ELECTRA: You are distressed, sir.

What is the matter? Why do you speak so strangely?

ORESTES: You are the lady Electra, are you not?

ELECTRA: I am, to my sorrow.

ORESTES: It is a pitiful story.

ELECTRA: Can it be pity for me, sir, that distresses you?

ORESTES: To be so foully wronged, so cursed by the gods.

ELECTRA: That's blasphemy, sir; but truly said of me.

ORESTES: Chained to this sad and solitary life.

ELECTRA: Sir, why do you gaze at me, and speak so sadly?

ORESTES: How little I knew till now of my own afflictions!

ELECTRA: What have we said that has enlightened you?

ORESTES: All that I see speaks of your load of hardship.

ELECTRA: You see but little of it.

ORESTES: Could there be more?

ELECTRA: A lodger in a house of murder –

ORESTES: Murder?

Of whom? What story is this?

ELECTRA: My father's murder;

And I the murderers' slave –

ORESTES: By whose compulsion?

ELECTRA: A mother's – in name, but nothing else, a mother.

ORESTES: What are her weapons? Force, privation?

ELECTRA: Both.

Force and privation, and malice of every kind.

ORESTES:

Is there no one to help you, no one to take your part?

ELECTRA:

None – but the one whose dust you have brought before me.

ORESTES: I see; and all that I see excites my pity,

My poor unhappy friend.

ELECTRA: No other man,

You may be sure, has ever pitied me.

ORESTES: No other man has ever come that knew

Your sorrows as his own.

ELECTRA: You come – can it be? –
As a kinsman? But from where?

ORESTES: Are these our friends?
If so, I could say more.

ELECTRA: Yes, they are friends,
They'll not betray you.

ORESTES: Give me back the urn,
Then I will tell you everything.

ELECTRA: No, no!
For pity's sake, don't ask me to do that!

ORESTES: Do as I say; believe me, it will be best.

ELECTRA: The only thing I love! ... Have pity, sir ...
Don't take it from me.

ORESTES: I cannot let you keep it.

ELECTRA: O am I never to lay you in your grave,
Orestes beloved?

ORESTES: You speak too rashly, lady;
This is no time for funerals.

ELECTRA: No time?
My brother dead –

ORESTES: You must not speak of that.

ELECTRA: Why must I not? Do even my dead disown me?

ORESTES: No one disowns you. And you need not weep.

ELECTRA: Not weep – over my brother's dust – not weep?

ORESTES: It is not his. It was all a masquerade.

ELECTRA:
Where is he then? Poor lad, where have they laid him?
Tell me, where is his grave?

ORESTES: There is no grave. Only the dead have graves.

ELECTRA: Dear lad, what are you saying?

ORESTES: Only the truth.

ELECTRA: He lives?

ORESTES: As I live.

ELECTRA: Is it really you?

ORESTES: Look – father's signet – do you believe me now?

ELECTRA: O light! O joy!

ORESTES: I share it.

ELECTRA: Is this indeed
  Your voice again?

ORESTES: Ask for no other witness.

ELECTRA: Your hand in mine?

ORESTES: For ever.

ELECTRA: Women, women!
  It is Orestes, look, women of Argos!
  His death was only a trick, and by that trick
  He has been given back to us!

CHORUS: We see,
  My dear, we see him and are ready to weep for joy.

ELECTRA: O brother darling,
  My darling's own son,
  Home at last,
  Brought home to me, to see me, find me here,
  As you have longed to find me!

ORESTES: Yes, I am here. But wait – say nothing yet.

ELECTRA: Why?

ORESTES: Better be silent. Someone inside might hear you.

ELECTRA: Ho, but I'm not afraid of them!
  By the Virgin Artemis, no, not afraid
  Of a houseful of good-for-nothings,
  Women!

ORESTES: Remember, women are sometimes warriors too.
  You have good cause to know it.

ELECTRA: O yes, yes . . .
  You bring it back to me . . .
  Nothing can hide,
  Nothing can take away
  Such sorrow as mine;

It will not let me go.

ORESTES: I know. But there will be a time and place
To remember what has happened.

ELECTRA: Time! Any time,
All time there is,
Will be the time
To say what must be said, and justly said,
Now that my lips are free.

ORESTES: They are. Be careful not to lose that freedom.

ELECTRA: How?

ORESTES: Say little, until the occasion gives you leave.

ELECTRA: Who could be silent at such a time,
Silent to greet your homecoming,
Brought back beyond all hope,
All dreaming?

ORESTES: I could not have come but in the gods' good time;
They brought me back to you.

ELECTRA: Better and better!
If the hand of God
Guided you back,
Back to this home of ours,
That is a sign
Heaven is working it out.

ORESTES: I would not curb your joy; but there is danger
In too much happiness.

ELECTRA: No, no!
You have come to make me happy
This long awaited day; you found me
Burdened with grief. O never, never —

ORESTES: What?

ELECTRA: Never leave me,
Never let me be parted
From your dear face.

ORESTES: He dies that would attempt it.

ELECTRA: Truly?

ORESTES: Believe me.

ELECTRA: O dear women, women, this is the voice
　　I never hoped to hear again.
　　How could I hear it, after all my suffering,
　　And lock my heart in silence
　　Or not shout for joy?
　　(To ORESTES)
　　You are with me now;
　　This is the dear dear face
　　Which I could not forget
　　Through all the sorrow of my life.

ORESTES: Say no more now.
　　The story of your mother's sins,
　　And of Aegisthus' crimes against our house,
　　His wild extravagance and wanton waste,
　　May keep till another time; 'twould take too long.
　　Now we must think, where to reveal ourselves,
　　Or where remain in hiding, in this campaign
　　To end the triumph of our enemies.
　　And remember, you must not let your mother see
　　A smile upon your face, when we go in;
　　Be weeping still, for my pretended death.
　　When we have won, there will be time to smile
　　And rejoice to your heart's content.

ELECTRA: Dear, I will do everything you ask me;
　　You are the cause of all my happiness,
　　I would not hinder you for all the world.
　　How could I fly in the face of the good genius
　　That serves us now?
　　You know – surely you know –
　　How things are here; Aegisthus is away,
　　Mother's at home; you need not be afraid
　　She'll ever see a smile upon my face;

Hatred has burned too deep in me for that.
I shall be weeping still, weeping for joy
At seeing you! To think you have come home
Twice in this hour, first dead and then alive!
How can I help my tears? It's all so strange –
If Father were to come back now alive,
I could believe that it was really he,
And not a ghost.
And now you've come like that,
So tell me what to do. Had I been left
To fight alone, I would have been content
With nothing less than victory with honour,
Or honourable death.

ORESTES: Hush! I can hear
Someone coming to the doors.

ELECTRA (*to* ORESTES *and* PYLADES, *as if to strangers*):
Come in, gentlemen.
Your gift is not of a gratifying kind
But cannot be refused acceptance.

The TUTOR *comes out of the palace.*

TUTOR: Have you taken leave of your senses, you two? Are
you so tired of life, or so short of commonsense you cannot
see you're standing on the brink of deadly danger, nay,
up to the neck in it already? If I hadn't been keeping a
sharp look-out behind the door all this time, your plans
might well have been in the house before you. Thank me
for saving you from that. It's time to stop all this speech-
making and everlasting jubilation, and come in. It's now or
never; delay is fatal in these affairs.

ORESTES: Is it safe for me to go in?

TUTOR: All's well. There's no chance of your being recognized.

ORESTES: You've told them I am dead?

TUTOR: As far as this house is concerned, you're dead and
buried.

ORESTES: What do they say? Are they glad of it?

TUTOR: I'll tell you that afterwards. For the present everything is as good – or as bad – as it can be.

ELECTRA: Who is this man, brother? Tell me, you must tell
me.

ORESTES: Don't you know?

ELECTRA: I cannot think –

ORESTES: Don't you remember into whose arms you once
entrusted me?

ELECTRA: Into whose arms? You mean –

ORESTES: Or by whose hands I was got safely away to
Phocis, as you had planned?

ELECTRA: Is this the man?
Is it he who was my only faithful friend
The day my father died?

ORESTES: This is the man.
No need for further question.

ELECTRA: O great day!
O friend, our house's only saviour – you –
It is really you, the man who has brought us two
Out of all our danger? O God bless those hands
And feet, for what they did for us! To think
That you were here so long, unrecognized,
With never a sign, bringing that awful news
Of death to torture me, and the lovely truth
Locked in your heart.
O I could call you father,
I look on you as one. Welcome, dear father.
Now I can tell you how I have hated you,
And loved you, more than any man alive,
All in a day.

TUTOR: You'd better say no more.
Of all that has happened, there will be nights in plenty,
Electra, and for every night a day,

To tell the story.
But it's to you two lads
That I must give the word for action.
Clytaemnestra's alone, with none but women near her.
Delay now, and you'll have to fight it out
With more and cleverer enemies.

ORESTES: Pylades,
There is no more time for talking. We must go in.
Salute my father's gods, whose shrines stand here
Before his doors.

They make salutations to the shrines, and go into the house.
ELECTRA *kneels to the statue of Apollo.*

ELECTRA: O Lord Apollo,
Hear them with mercy, and hear my prayer too.
As I have often visited thee
With such poor offerings as my means afforded,
So now, with all I have
Of reverence and supplication,
I humbly pray and beseech thee for aid and favour
In what we now intend;
That thou mayst show to men
With what bountiful wages the gods reward the wicked.

She goes into the house.

CHORUS:
Watch now; battle and lust of blood
Move onward step by step
To the inevitable end.
There go the hunters into the house,
The hounds on the trail of the evil-doers.
There is no escaping.
Our dream's fulfilment cannot be long delayed.

Now the defender of the dead
Creeps into his father's house,

The old rich house,
With a sword sharpened for blood. Hermes,
Who found the way and kept it secret,
The son of Maia,
Leads him on to the end; the waiting is over.

ELECTRA *comes out.*

ELECTRA: Listen, women. In a moment now
The men will do it. Wait in silence.

CHORUS: What are they doing?

ELECTRA: Standing behind her
While she prepares the urn for burial.

CHORUS: Why have you come out?

ELECTRA: To watch for Aegisthus,
In case he takes us by surprise.

They wait in silent suspense; until the voice
of CLYTAEMNESTRA *is heard.*

CLYTAEMNESTRA:
Help! Death is upon us! Is there no one to help?

ELECTRA: There it is. Do you hear, do you hear?

CHORUS: O what terrible cries!

CLYTAEMNESTRA:
Have mercy, my son, have mercy on your mother!

ELECTRA (*shouting through the closed doors*):
You had none for him, nor for his father before him!

CHORUS: Now may the house and kingdom cry:
This is the end, the end of the days of affliction!

CLYTAEMNESTRA: Ah! . . .

ELECTRA: Strike her again, strike!

CLYTAEMNESTRA: Ah! . . .

ELECTRA: May Aegisthus suffer the same!

CHORUS:
The curse has its way;
The dead speak from the earth;
The tide is turned and the blood

Is sucked from the slayer
By the slain of long ago.

    (ORESTES *and* PYLADES *come out of the house.*)

Here they come. Their hands are red
With the blood of the sacrifice. And who
Condemns? Not I.

ELECTRA: All right?

ORESTES: All right . . . if Apollo was right.

ELECTRA: Did you kill the wretch?

ORESTES: You'll have no more indignities
    To suffer from her.

CHORUS: Take care. I can see Aegisthus.

ELECTRA: Go back!

ORESTES: Where is he?

ELECTRA: Just turning out of the street,
    Suspecting nothing.
    He will soon be here.

CHORUS: Quick – go back into the hall;
    And may all go as well as before.

ORESTES: Trust us for that.

ELECTRA: Go, go.

ORESTES: We'll go.

ELECTRA: I'll meet him here.

    ORESTES *and* PYLADES *go back into the house.*

CHORUS: You must give him a friendly greeting
    To lure him unsuspecting
    To his reckoning with justice.

        Enter AEGISTHUS *from the town.*

AEGISTHUS:
They tell me some Phocian visitors have been here
With a story of Orestes' having lost his life
In a chariot-smash. Does anyone know where they are?
           (*Silence*)

Electra, what have you to say? ... Have you lost your
    tongue?
You were not used to be so modest. He's your brother ...
You must know something; you had better tell me about it.

ELECTRA:
Of course, I know all about it. It's my duty to know
All that is happening to my nearest and dearest.

AEGISTHUS: Where are the messengers, then?

ELECTRA: They are in the house.
They have paid their respects to the mistress.

AEGISTHUS: What is their message?
Do they say he is really dead?

ELECTRA: They not only say it,
They have shown us the proof.

AEGISTHUS: Can I see it for myself?

ELECTRA: Yes, you can see it. It's not a pretty sight.

AEGISTHUS:
This is good news – the best you have given me yet.

ELECTRA: I wish you joy of it – if you find it so.

AEGISTHUS:
Enough then. Open the doors! Let all my people
See this sight. And fools who fixed their hopes
On this poor creature, when they see his corpse,
May now accept my yoke, and not require
My whip to humble them.

ELECTRA: I need no teaching.
I have learned my lesson at last, learned how to serve
The will of those who have the upper hand.

The Palace doors are opened, disclosing ORESTES *and* PYLADES
standing beside the body of CLYTAEMNESTRA. *The body is
covered.* AEGISTHUS *goes up and looks at it for a moment in
silence.*

AEGISTHUS: Surely, O God, there is example here
Of righteous retribution. If it be so,

In the presence of Nemesis, let me say no more.
Uncover the face, for I must mourn my kindred.
ORESTES: You, sir, not I, should lift this veil, and look
On what lies here, and make your kind farewell.
AEGISTHUS:
True. So I will. (*To* ELECTRA) Call Clytaemnestra here,
If she is in the house.
ORESTES: She is near you now,
Not far to seek.

           AEGISTHUS *uncovers the body.*

AEGISTHUS: God, what is this?
ORESTES: Afraid?
Of whom? Strangers?
AEGISTHUS: Whose trap is this
That I have fallen into?
ORESTES: Are you so blind
You cannot tell the living from the dead?
AEGISTHUS: God help me, now I know. You are Orestes.
ORESTES: The prophet's eyes are opened.
AEGISTHUS: This is the end ...
Yet let me say one thing –
ELECTRA: Let him say nothing!
For God's sake, brother, do not listen to him!
When a man's hour has come, a little grace
Can do him little good. Kill him at once,
And throw his body to the gravediggers
That wait on such as he, out of our sight.
No other punishment can pay his debt
For all that I have suffered.
ORESTES (*to* AEGISTHUS): Go inside.
Words cannot settle the account between us,
Only your life.
AEGISTHUS: Why must I go in there?
Must this good deed be hidden from the daylight?

Strike, and have done with it.

ORESTES: I give the orders.
  Go to the place in which you killed my father;
  There you shall die.

AEGISTHUS: Must this roof see
  The sorrows of Pelops age after age repeated
  To the end of time?

ORESTES: It shall see yours, I prophesy.

AEGISTHUS:
  That's more foreknowledge than your father owned.

ORESTES: You have an answer to everything. Come now,
  We're wasting time.

AEGISTHUS: Lead on, then.

ORESTES: You go first.

AEGISTHUS: Afraid I'll cheat you?

ORESTES: You might think to choose
  An easier death. I mean to see you suffer
  Up to the hilt. Could this swift justice, death,
  Take all who choose to step across the law,
  Law would be less defied.

   AEGISTHUS *goes in;* ORESTES *and* PYLADES *follow;*
                     the doors are shut.

CHORUS: Now for the House of Atreus
  Freedom is won
  From all her suffering,
  And this day's work well done.

                  EXEUNT

WOMEN OF TRACHIS

Some time after the performance of his famous labours in the service of Eurystheus, Heracles married Deianeira, daughter of Oineus of Calydon, whom he won after a trial of strength with a rival suitor, the river-god Achelous. Still other tasks were in store for him, and while Deianeira made her home at Trachis, on the Malian Gulf, Heracles was continually engaged in various quests which took him from her side.

At the opening of the play, after an absence of fifteen months, his return is anxiously awaited by Deianeira, for the oracles have declared that the time has now come when he is to find rest and an end of his labours. This prediction Deianeira herself brings to a tragic fulfilment when, in her desire to hasten his coming and recapture his errant love, she unwittingly prepares disaster both for herself and her husband.

WOMEN OF TRACHIS

*

CHARACTERS

Deianeira, *the wife of Heracles*
Hyllus, *their son*
Heracles
Lichas, *a herald*
A Nurse
A Messenger
An old Man
Chorus of Women of Trachis

*

The scene is before the house of Heracles at Trachis, in Greece.

DEIANEIRA *comes out of the house, attended by the Nurse.*

DEIANEIRA: Call no man happy, unhappy . . . you cannot tell
Till the day of his death. The proverb is old and plain.
It may be true. I know I'm still alive
And I have had sorrow and suffering in plenty.
When I was a girl at home
In Pleuron where my father Oineus lived,
I dreaded marriage, dreaded it more than any
Of all the girls I knew.
I was wooed by the god of a river, the river Achelous.
He used to come in different guises
To ask my father for his consent.
He had three shapes:
Sometimes he came as a bull,
Sometimes a gleaming writhing snake,
Sometimes a man with a bull's forehead,
Cascades of river water falling

Down his thick dark beard.
This was the husband I had to look forward to;
No wonder I was always praying for death
Rather than give myself to such a master.
Then, to my joy, came Heracles,
The splendid son of Zeus and of Alcmena.
He fought with the monster and delivered me from him.
What kind of a battle it was, I cannot tell you;
I never knew. If there was anyone
That could sit and watch that spectacle,
He is the one who could describe it for you.
I could only hide my head in terror,
Wondering if I should have to pay
The price of my beauty in a life of misery.
But the God of Battles brought it to a happy issue.
Was it so happy?
Heracles chose me for his wife; and since that day
I have had no moment's rest from fear
On his account.
Each night's new terror drives away
The terror of the night before.
We had children . . . but he never sees them
Except as a farmer sees a distant field
On the edge of his estate, visiting it
Now and again, at planting or at harvest.
That's what his life has been,
Home one minute and away the next,
A slave to his employer.

And now that he has won his freedom, now
My trial is worse than ever.
His last encounter was with Iphitus;
He overpowered and killed him, and since then
Trachis has been our home, an exile's home,

By permission of a generous foreign lord.
But where my husband is, who knows? The agony I suffer
Is all I have in place of him.
Something has happened to him. I almost know
Something has happened to him; it's not a day,
A week, but ten months – more, five more than that,
And not a word of him. Something has happened to him.
He left a writing before he went away;
I knew what it meant – and yet I prayed,
How often I prayed there might be nothing bad in it!

NURSE: Come now, mistress Deianeira; in tears again
For your husband's absence – how often have I seen you so.
If a servant, a slave, may advise a freeborn mistress,
I must tell you something for your good.
You've plenty of sons; why not send one of them
To find your husband? Hyllus would be the best.
He's the one should go, if any thought
Of his father's safety ever troubled him.
I see him coming this minute. Now's the time,
If you agree with my advice, to take it –
And here he is.

Enter HYLLUS.

DEIANEIRA: Hyllus, my son,
I've just been learning that words of wisdom may fall
From humble lips. Our good slave here
Has spoken like the best of us.

HYLLUS: What has she said, mother?
If it is for me to hear.

DEIANEIRA: Since your father has been so long a stranger,
That you should make no search for him, she says,
Does you no credit.

HYLLUS: I know where he is,
If rumour can be trusted.

DEIANEIRA: What have you heard?

Where do they say he is?

HYLLUS: They say he has been a Lydian woman's slave
This whole year past –

DEIANEIRA: Can it be true!
If he could bring himself to that,
Then nothing is impossible.

HYLLUS: But now, I hear, he is free from that subjection.

DEIANEIRA: Where do they say he is, then? Alive or dead?

HYLLUS: Waging a war – or on the point of doing so –
Against Euboea, where Eurytus is king.

DEIANEIRA:
Euboea? My son, do you know that when he left us
He gave me an oracle about that place?

HYLLUS: What was that, mother? I never heard of it.

DEIANEIRA: It said that either he should meet with death,
Or this would be his last exploit
And he would live in peace henceforth
Till his life's end. O Hyllus, Hyllus,
His fate is in the balance: will you not go,
And try to help him? If he lives, we live;
And if he dies, we die.

HYLLUS: Of course I will go, mother.
If only I had known of this oracle before,
I would have gone to find him long ago.
He was always so fortunate, I never thought of fear
Or anxiety for him. Now that I know this much,
I will do anything to find out all the truth.

DEIANEIRA:
Then go, my dear. Good news is well worth having,
And better late than never.

> HYLLUS *goes into the house.*
> *Enter the* CHORUS *of women of Trachis.*

CHORUS:
O Sun, whose birth makes pale the starry eyes

Of Night, thy mother; at whose bed
She watches when the fires burn low;
Great Lord of Light, we ask to know
Where Heracles, Alcmena's son, now lies,
On either coast, or on the seas that flow
Between the continents. Shine out and show,
All-seeing Eye, where he has laid his head.

Here Deianeira, vainly sorrowing –
A bird bereft – his captive wife –
In agony and endless tears
Watches wide-eyed the unsleeping fears
That haunt her lonely bed, remembering
Her absent husband and the empty years
Of her long widowhood. No comfort cheers,
Or hope of happiness, her drooping life.

To and fro, like the waves in endless restless motion
Driven by winds from north and south in billowing tides,
The scion of Cadmus, tossed on a Cretan ocean
Of troubled life, now sinks in the trough, now rides
The crest of the wave; but the god that guides
His feet from the door of death, has saved him from
        perdition.

Lady, we honour your grief, but cannot think it prudent
To kill the root of hope; for the god that governs all
Has given to no man life without chastisement
Of pain, yet pain and joy alternate fall
As sure as the perennial
Rotation of the Great Bear in the high firmament.

Nothing abides; the starry night,
Our wealth, our sorrows, pass away.
Tomorrow another has his day
Of happiness, of disappointment.

Build on this thought your hopes,
Most noble lady; can Zeus forget
To care for any of his sons?

DEIANEIRA: I see you know the cause of my distress;
You cannot know – and pray you may never know
How deep it eats into my heart. Young things
Grow in their own place, sheltered from the sun,
Sheltered from rain, from wind – a pleasant life,
Untroubled. But when she that was a maid
Must take the name of wife, she takes a burden
Of nightmare terrors, suffering for husband or children.
Any woman who has known this, will know
What kind of thing I suffer.
And what I am going to speak of is only one
Of the many griefs I have known, and yet the worst.
The last time when my husband went away,
He left behind him an ancient tablet, inscribed
With certain signs, whose meaning he had never dared,
Before any of his previous journeys, to explain to me.
He had always gone out as if he meant to win,
Not as if going to his death.
This time, as one speaking from the grave, he told me
What share of his estate I should have as his dowager,
And how he had divided his land among his sons,
Fixing the exact time – a year and three months
From the day of his going out; that day, he said,
Would be either his last on earth, or else the beginning
Of peaceful days for the rest of his mortal life.
Thus, he said, it was the will of the immortal gods
That the labours of Heracles should be brought to an end;
Thus it had been spoken at Dodona by the ancient oak
Long ago, by the voice of the two dove-priestesses.
And now that moment is here, and the fulfilment must
come.

That is why my sleep is broken, and I start to tremble
At the thought of losing him, the greatest man
The world has ever seen.

CHORUS: Hush, Deianeira.
Someone is coming . . . a man with his head garlanded,
A sign of good news.

The MESSENGER, *an old man, enters.*

MESSENGER: Mistress Deianeira, I have the honour to be
The first to bring you the news that puts an end
To all your fears.
Heracles is alive, has won his victory,
And is coming back to bring the spoils of battle
Home to our country's gods.

DEIANEIRA: What? What do you say, sir?

MESSENGER:
Your honourable husband is coming home to you
And you will see his triumph.

DEIANEIRA: Has one of our people
Or some stranger told you this?

MESSENGER: Lichas our herald is crying the news
To a listening crowd, down in the summer pasture.
When I heard it, I ran to be the first to tell you,
Hoping for your thanks, and maybe some reward.

DEIANEIRA:
Why didn't he come himself, if his news is good?

MESSENGER:
That's not so easy for him, my lady. He's surrounded
By the whole of Trachis, testing him with questions.
He cannot move a foot; everyone has something to ask
And won't let him go till it's answered. So there he is,
Willy or nilly, as long as they like to keep him.
You'll see him presently, though.

DEIANEIRA: O God of Oeta's virgin fields,
At long last you have given me happiness!

Sing, women in the house, and friends beyond our gates!
Sing for this harvest of light, this dawn of joy
That ends our dreams in gladness!

CHORUS:
Now let the house be filled
With maiden voices singing at the hearth
For joy; and let the shouts of men together
Praise the bright arrow-armed
Apollo, our defender!

Sing, women, sing to Artemis,
Apollo's sister, huntress of the deer,
The fire-encircled; praise
Her neighbour-nymphs!

O master of my soul,
I float on air, the sweet
Music of flutes would win me now,
And twining ivy-tendrils whirl me round
In Bacchanalian dance.
Paean! Paean!
        (*They dance in joyful abandon, until one of them breaks
                off, seeing persons approaching.*)
Look, look, my lady!
Here is good news in person
Before your very eyes.

DEIANEIRA: I see them, friends; even my weary eyes
Are not such sleepy sentinels as to miss
That company approaching ...
                (LICHAS, *the herald, enters, accompanied by
                        several captive women*).
Welcome at last, good herald – if good news
Is what you bring.

LICHAS: My lady, it is good to be here, and good to receive
The kindly greeting which befits our service.

When fortune is kind, kind words are welcome too.

DEIANEIRA:

Good friend, first tell me the thing I first must hear –
Shall I see Heracles alive?

LICHAS: He was alive
And fit and well and sound in every limb
When last I saw him.

DEIANEIRA: Where was that?
On his own or foreign soil? Where was it?

LICHAS: In Euboea, on the headland called Cenaeum,
He is dedicating an altar to the god they worship there,
With offerings of the first-fruits of the land.

DEIANEIRA: Was this for the fulfilment of a vow,
Or on the instruction of some oracle?

LICHAS: A vow, made when he set out to destroy
The country of these women you see before you.

DEIANEIRA:

Poor things ... who are they? and whose prisoners?
If they're as unhappy as they look
I'm sorry for them.

LICHAS: They are your husband's captives,
Taken from the city of Eurytus, to be his prize
And chosen offerings to the gods.

DEIANEIRA: All this long time ... fighting against that city?
One would not have thought it possible ... so many days
I have quite lost count.

LICHAS: Ah no. Not all that time.
The greater part of it he spent among
The Lydians, detained, he says, against his will,
Deprived of freedom, a sold slave. Nothing to be ashamed of,
My lady, when Zeus was the contriver of it.
Yes, he was sold in bondage to Omphale,
A barbarian mistress; and so a whole year passed.
He told us so himself. The humiliation

So stung him that he swore a solemn oath
Never to rest until he had made a slave
Of the man whose act had brought him to this plight –
His wife and children too. That was his oath;
And he was as good as his word; freed and absolved,
He gathered about him an army of foreigners
And marched against the land of Eurytus –
For he was the one and only mortal man
He held responsible for that affair.
It came about like this. Heracles had come
As a guest to Eurytus – they were old acquaintances –
But Eurytus took occasion to sneer at him
With open insults and malicious intent.
'You with your charmed infallible arrows!' he said.
'My sons could give you points at archery.
You're nothing better than a down-trodden slave,
A free man's property!' One day, at a banquet,
When Heracles was drunk with wine, they took him
And threw him out of doors. He had his revenge
When Iphitus came, in search of straying horses,
To the hill of Tiryns; Heracles waylaid him,
His thoughts being somewhere other than his eyes,
And hurled him over the edge of a precipice.
The Almighty Father punished him for that
By having him sold like any common slave
And banished from the country. He was angry with him
For having killed a man by treachery –
The first and only time. Had he fought fair,
And won the day, Zeus would have surely pardoned him
And called his triumph just. The gods hate insolence
As much as we.
So all those arrogant folk,
With their uncivil tongues, have gone to their place
In Hades, and their city become a slave-mart.

And here, as you see, are some of their womenfolk
Exchanging happiness for a taste of misery.
It was his command, which I am faithfully performing,
That they should be brought here to you. Himself
You may expect to see, as soon as he has given
Thank-offerings for victory to Zeus, his father.
And that, I think, will be the most welcome part
Of all these happy tidings.

CHORUS: O lady, this is your day of success!
Your joy must be complete, both in the present news
And what he promises.

DEIANEIRA: Yes, I have every reason to be happy
From the bottom of my heart, at this success.
Good fortune, and happiness, they must go together ...
And yet ... if we are not blind, we cannot but fear
Today's success may be tomorrow's fall ...
My friends, I am full of pity at this sad sight,
These poor unhappy exiles, homeless, fatherless,
Waifs in a strange land – daughters of free-born families,
For all we know, and now condemned to slavery.
Zeus, Giver of Victory,
May you never deal thus with any child of mine,
Or may I die before that day!
This sight is horror enough.

        (*To one of the prisoners, a young girl*)

Whose daughter are you, poor child?
Are you married? A mother, perhaps?
No, neither, from your looks, I think.
But well-born, surely ... Lichas, whose daughter is she?
I think I am sorrier for her than all the rest,
She seems the most sensitive of her condition.
Do you know who her parents are? Tell me if you do.

LICHAS: I don't, my lady. How should I? But very likely
She comes from not the lowest of their houses.

DEIANEIRA:

Do you mean . . . the king's? Can she be Eurytus' child?

LICHAS: I couldn't say. I haven't asked any questions.

DEIANEIRA:

Have none of the others mentioned her name to you?

LICHAS: Never, my lady. It wasn't my business to talk to them.

DEIANEIRA:

Come, child, you'll tell me, won't you? I should be sorry
Not to be able to call you by your name.

LICHAS:

I shall be surprised, my lady, if you can get her to speak.
She's never uttered a syllable all this time,
Being so much overcome by the weight of her troubles,
Weeping continually, poor girl, ever since she was parted
From her homeland's windy sky. It'll do her no good
To be so sullen; but one can understand it.

DEIANEIRA:

Let us not trouble her, then. If she will not speak,
Let her go in. She has sorrows enough to bear,
And I must not add to them.
Let us all go in; then you can be on your way,
And I will attend to what is necessary here.

> LICHAS *and the prisoners begin to move towards the house.*
> *The* MESSENGER *draws* DEIANEIRA *aside.*

MESSENGER:

My lady, if you will stay a moment, when these are gone,
I can tell you something about your visitors.
There is something you should know, which has not been
    told you yet,
And I know all the truth of it.

DEIANEIRA: What is the matter, sir?

I cannot stay —

MESSENGER: Please listen a moment, my lady.
My first news turned out true, and so will this.

DEIANEIRA: Do you want me to call the others back,
Or is it to me and my friends that you wish to speak?

MESSENGER:
You and your friends will do. Never mind the others.

DEIANEIRA:
Well, they are gone. Let us hear what you have to say.

MESSENGER:
That man's a liar. The last thing that he told you
Was not all fair and square, by any means.
Either he's playing some sharp game now, or else
His first report was some way from the truth.

DEIANEIRA:
I don't understand. Please tell me what you mean.

MESSENGER:
He told me – and many others were there to hear him –
That it was all on account of that girl you were speaking to
That your husband went and slew King Eurytus
And sacked his fortress city, Oechalia.
If any god inspired him in that great exploit,
It was Eros, no other; and it had nothing to do
With his slavery to the Lydian woman, Omphale,
Nor his hurling Iphitus over a precipice.
It seems your husband, unable to persuade the father
To let him have his girl for a concubine,
Trumps up some trifling charge by way of excuse,
Attacks her country, where Eurytus – that's her father –
Is king, kills him, and lays the city to ruins.
Then back he comes, sending her home before him,
With proper ceremony, you see, my lady,
Not as a slave – oh dear me, no – not likely,
Seeing he's head over heels in love with her . . .
I thought I'd better tell you all, my lady,
Just as he told it in the market-place at Trachis.
There were plenty besides that heard him, as well as me:

They'll tell you the same . . . If I've said more than I should,
I'm sorry . . . but I've spoken nothing but the truth.

DEIANEIRA: O God, what am I to do!
What devil in disguise have I let in
To wreck my happiness? A nameless girl
Her escort called her.

MESSENGER: Nay, a famous name,
And famous beauty!
Eurytus' daughter, they called her Iole.
And Lichas couldn't tell you who she was,
Because he never asked!

CHORUS: Cursed above all ill-doers
Is he that practises base cunning and deceit!

DEIANEIRA: Friends, what am I to do?
This news has shocked me utterly.

CHORUS: Go and ask Lichas; he may tell you the truth
If you insist.

DEIANEIRA: Yes, that would be best. I will.

MESSENGER: Do you want me to stay, my lady?

DEIANEIRA: Yes, stay. (LICHAS *appears at the house door*.)
He's coming of his own accord, without my sending
For him.

LICHAS: Is there any message, my lady, for me to take
To Heracles? Command me, I am on my way.

DEIANEIRA: We waited a long time for your coming, sir.
Must you hurry away without another word?

LICHAS: If you have anything to ask, I am here to answer it.

DEIANEIRA: And will you answer truthfully?

LICHAS: Ay, by Zeus,
If it is anything I know.

DEIANEIRA; Who is that girl you brought here?

LICHAS: A Euboean girl. I don't know where she came from.

MESSENGER: Look here, young man. Do you know whom
you're talking to?

LICHAS: What do you mean?

MESSENGER: Answer, you understand me.

LICHAS: To the lady Deianeira – if I can trust my eyes –
Daughter of Oineus and wife of Heracles,
My honoured mistress.

MESSENGER: That's what I wanted to hear.
You acknowledge that you are her subject?

LICHAS: Such is my duty.

MESSENGER: Then how if we find you guilty
Of failing in your duty? What punishment will you deserve?

LICHAS: How should I fail? . . . What sort of a trick is this?

MESSENGER: No trick at all – except the one you're playing.

LICHAS: I'm going. I was a fool to listen to so much talk.

MESSENGER: Not till you have answered one plain question.

LICHAS: Ask it;
You've got a tongue in your head.

MESSENGER: About this prisoner
You've just brought home – you know which one I mean –

LICHAS: I dare say I do. What of her?

MESSENGER: Did you not say
That this same girl, whom now you deny all knowledge of,
Was entrusted to you as Iole, daughter of Eurytus?

LICHAS: Who heard me say it? Who and where is the man
That will testify to hearing me say such a thing?

MESSENGER: Hundreds of people. There in the market square
In the town of Trachis a huge crowd heard you say it.

LICHAS:
Ay, thought they heard it, maybe. To give an opinion
Is a different thing from proving the actual words.

MESSENGER: An opinion indeed! You said – and you took
your oath on it –
This girl you had got was the bride of Heracles.

LICHAS:
I called her his bride? For the love of God, dear mistress,

Who is this fellow?

MESSENGER: This fellow is one who heard,
   From your own mouth, that the utter destruction of a city
   Was a labour of love, love for this very girl,
   No consequence of the Lydian affair – just love,
   The love that this girl inspired.

LICHAS: Let him go, my lady;
   No one in his senses should bandy words with a madman.

DEIANEIRA:
   By the fires of God that flame on the high hill-forests,
   Give me the truth! I am not so meanly made.
   Do you think I do not know that the heart of man
   Can change in its affections? Only a fool
   Would try conclusions with the God of Love.
   Love has his own way with the gods themselves:
   Why not with me? Why not with another woman,
   As much a woman as I? It would be madness
   To blame my husband for catching this infection,
   Or blame the woman, his partner in a thing
   That is no disgrace to them, no offence to me.
   I shall not blame them . . . But your prevarication –
   That was not right. If it was he that taught you,
   He did not teach you well. If it was your own –
   No doubt you meant well – but in the end, you see,
   You'll prove more cruel than kind . . . Now tell me the truth.
   The name of liar is a brand of infamy
   To a free-born man. Nor is it possible
   To cover up your tracks; your many hearers
   Will tell me all you said . . . Don't be afraid;
   There's nothing to be afraid of. Not to be told
   Would hurt me deeply; but to know the truth,
   That can't be terrible. This is not the first . . .
   No man has loved more women than Heracles.
   I've never blamed or scolded any of them –

Nor this one, though she be melted heart and soul
In the fire of her love; because I am sorry for her;
As soon as I saw her I was sorry for her
Because her beauty has been her ruin, and she,
Unwittingly, has brought her country down
To slavery and destruction ... Let the stream run on,
And the wind blow where it will ...
Now, sir, once more,
Whomever else you may deceive, tell me the truth.

CHORUS: It is good advice; obey her; she will be grateful,
As we shall too.

LICHAS: So be it, my honoured mistress.
Now that I see you look with human eyes
On human weakness, not without charity,
I will tell the whole truth and keep nothing back.
It is just as this man said; this *is* the woman
For whom that violent passion conquered the heart
Of Heracles, and it is on her account
Her father's city, Oechalia, now lies ruined
In the devastation of war. Nor did your husband –
To his credit it must be said – ever deny it,
Or ask me to conceal it; that was my doing;
I shrank from grieving you with such a story.
The fault was mine, if such you call it. So,
Now you have all the truth, may I say, my lady,
Both for your sake and hers, it would be best
That you should bear with her, and be resolved
To abide by what you just now said of her.
Great are the victories of Heracles –
But here, in love, he met his match.

DEIANEIRA: I *am* resolved to do as you advise;
I have no mind to add to my afflictions
By taking arms against the gods. Come in,
And you shall take my messages, and gifts –

Gifts in return for gifts, as is most right –
You shall take them too; you came so richly attended,
It will not do to let you go away
With nothing in your hands.

They go into the house.

CHORUS:

O great and unconquerable Aphrodite –
Hers is the power and hers the victory
In every battlefield. We know
Gods have bowed down before her – three,
The King of Heaven, the Prince of murky Death,
The Master of the earth-shaking sea.
So here, in mortal strife,
Two valiant champions in the lists,
With dusty feet and flying fists,
Wrestled to win a wife.

One, God of a river, great Achelous,
In shape a huge high-horned four-footed bull,
Came down from Oeneadae,
The other from the citadel
That Bacchus loves – from Thebes – the son of Zeus
With spear and club invincible
And springing bow, to fight
With fierce desire; and there between
As umpire stood the Cyprian, Queen
Of love's delight.

Hammer of fists and bowstring twanging,
Clatter of horn and club, arms grappling,
Thunder-blows on foreheads pounding,
Deep breasts groaning. And far away
The fair one waiting on the hillside,
Waiting
To greet her husband . . .

They fought, and their battle-prize,
The bride so beautiful,
Waited in agony . . .
So soon a mother must lose
Her tender lamb.

After a short pause, DEIANEIRA *comes out of the house. She
has with her a small casket, closed and sealed.*

DEIANEIRA: Now, friends, our visitor is saying farewell
To the captive women, and I have slipped away
To tell you about a plan I have in hand,
Also to share my sorry state with you . . .
To have to welcome into my house a girl –
No virgin either, I should guess – a baggage
Thrust on me like a cargo on a ship
To wreck my peace of mind! The two of us
Under one blanket, wrapped in one lover's arms!
This is my good and faithful husband's gratitude,
My pay for keeping house and home for him
All these long years . . . I cannot be angry with him,
His nature is too much prone to this disorder.
But share the house with her, and share the husband –
It's more than any woman can do . . . I know,
I see how it is: the one with youthful beauty
Ripening to its prime, the other falling away.
The eye must ever enjoy the flower, the feet
Turn from the withered stalk. This is my fear,
Heracles to be called my *husband,* but her *man* . . .
But there, as I said, a woman must have more sense
Than to cherish anger . . . Let me tell you, my friends,
Of the means by which I hope to find relief
And remedy for this affliction. A precious gift
Was given me long ago by a monstrous creature
Of untold age, the long-haired centaur, Nessus.

No more than a child, I took it as he lay dying,
A salve from his blood. It was he that carried men,
For payment, across the torrent of Evenus,
In his arms, without oar or sail. He carried me,
The day I first went out from my father's house
As the wife of Heracles. I rode on his shoulders;
But in mid-stream, he grossly handled me,
And at my cries the son of Zeus turned round
And shot an arrow which pierced him through the lungs.
These were the Centaur's dying words: 'Dear child,
Old Oineus' daughter, listen, and this shall be
Your gain from riding over the river with me,
Last of my passengers: preserve the blood
That clots around the arrow-head, envenomed
With black bane from the Lernaean Hydra's gall.
This charm will bind the heart of Heracles
If ever he should look upon a woman
To love her more than you.' So I remembered
This gift, which I have kept, locked safe away,
Since Nessus died; and I have here a tunic
Dipped in the salve, and treated as he prescribed
Before he breathed his last. So all is ready . . .
O God preserve me from any sinful deed,
Or from the knowledge of any, as I abhor
The woman that would stoop to such a thing!
But if by love-charms I could vanquish *her*,
And put a spell to work on Heracles –
Well, there it is . . . Have I done foolishly? If so,
I'll think no more of it.

CHORUS: Why no; if you believe some good will come of it,
We think you have done well.

DEIANEIRA: Yes, I believe . . .
There is every chance – but the proof is yet to be seen.

CHORUS: Well, only trial can show it. Without experience

You cannot know, but only guess the truth.

DEIANEIRA: Then we must try it. Here is our messenger,
Ready to go. But keep my secret close.
If there is any shame, it need not be known,
If proper caution be observed.

             LICHAS has now come out of the house.

LICHAS: My lady, I have already overstayed my time
And should be going. You have instructions for me?

DEIANEIRA:
Yes, Lichas. I have been getting something ready
While you were talking to the women in the house.
Here is a tunic, a present for my husband,
Of my own hand's making. Take it to him, please.
And when you give it to him, tell him this:
No one but he must put it on, or touch it;
Nor must it be exposed to the light of the sun,
Nor fire in a sacred place, nor at the hearth,
Until he wears it on a holy day,
Standing before the altar of sacrifice,
For all to see and marvel at its beauty.
This was my vow, that on his safe homecoming,
Or news of his coming, I would have him wear
This garment of honour, appearing before the gods
Arrayed as never before, to do them service.
This seal upon the box – my signet's mark –
Is a token which he will recognize. Now go.
Two things to remember: first, that messengers
Should never try to better their instructions;
Second, that what you do, if faithfully done,
You do for both of us, and both will thank you.

LICHAS: My lady, on the word of a faithful follower
Of the craft of Hermes, I shall do your errand
Without a slip, to deliver safe and sound
This casket and your message word for word.

DEIANEIRA: Then that is all. How things are here, you know;
I need not tell you what to say.

LICHAS: I know. I'll tell him all is well.

DEIANEIRA: And how his little friend was welcomed here,
How glad I was to see her.

LICHAS: It was a touching sight, my lady.

DEIANEIRA:
There's nothing more he'll want to know. My love ...
But maybe it's too soon to speak of that,
Before we know he needs it.

LICHAS *takes his leave.* DEIANEIRA *goes
into the house.*

CHORUS:
Hear this, all men that dwell beside
The warm springs gushing from the rocks,
And on the margin of the sea
Beneath high Oeta, by the gulf
Of Malis, on the land well-loved
By Artemis, the golden huntress,
Sacred shore where Hellas holds
The synod of Thermopylae.

For you sweet flutes shall sing,
Not sorrow's woeful tune,
But lyric melodies
Of heavenly joy, to bring
Alcmena's son, the son of Zeus,
Home proudly carrying
The spoils of all his victories.

Twelve months we waited for his coming,
We thought him lost, we had no word,
The sea had taken him; and she,
His faithful wife, her poor heart breaking,
Wept all her life away. But now

The War-god is awake, the sword
Unsheathed to cut the knots that bound
The dark days of her misery.

O bring him, bring him; rest not,
Strong ship, swift oars, until
His journey's over; bring him
Home from the island shrine
Where now he worships. Bring him
Charmed by the magic medicine,
The Centaur's spell,
Steeping his senses in desire.

DEIANEIRA *comes out of the house.*

DEIANEIRA:
O my friends, I begin to be afraid of what I have done.
If I have gone too far –
CHORUS: Has anything happened, my lady?
DEIANEIRA:
Nothing that I know; but my heart sinks at the thought
Of the victory I had hoped for turning to great disaster.
CHORUS: Is it about the gift you sent to Heracles?
DEIANEIRA:
The tunic; yes. O let it be a warning to everyone
Not to rush blindly into an act whose consequence
Cannot be foreseen!
CHORUS: Tell us, if you can, my lady,
What it is that makes you afraid.
DEIANEIRA: Something has happened . . .
When you hear, you will say it is a miracle beyond belief.
A knot of sheep's wool, which I had used just now
To anoint the robe, has vanished into nothing!
No one destroyed it, it consumed away of itself
And crumbled where it lay on a surface of stone.
But first I must tell you exactly how it happened,

Then you'll know all.
The instructions the Centaur gave me,
As he lay with the deadly arrow in his side,
Were graved on my memory, as if inscribed on bronze
Indelible, and I obeyed them all to the letter:
To keep the salve concealed in some safe place,
To keep it away from fire, and not to expose it
To the light and heat of the sun, but leave it untouched
Until the time should come to use the unguent
As need should require. All this I did. And now,
When the moment came, I plucked a handful of fleece
From our own flocks here, and took it into the house
Where none could see, and daubed the robe with it;
Then wrapped it carefully, keeping it from the sun,
And placed it in the casket which you saw.
As I went back just now into the house,
I saw this thing I shudder to describe,
A thing beyond all human understanding –
I must have thrown away the knot of wool
With which I smeared the robe, into the glare
Of the scorching sun, and as it took the heat
It crumbled to nothing, shrivelled into powder,
And there it lay, scattered upon the soil
Like so much sawdust blown from a woodman's bench.
But out of the earth it fell on, foamy bubbles
Came oozing up, like the fermenting juice
Of blue-ripe grapes crushed out upon the ground.
So now I am at my wits' end. What I have done
Must have some deadly consequence. O why,
Why should I think the monster at his death
Would wish to do me good, who caused his death?
Far from it, he was only duping me
To bring about the death of his assailant.
Now I have learnt the truth, it is too late,

Too late – my own act will have caused his death,
If what I think is true. That fatal arrow,
I know, had wounded the immortal Cheiron;
It kills whatever it touches, man or beast.
That same black venom in the blood of Nessus
That issued from his wound, will now kill Heracles.
It will ... it must ... I know it cannot fail.
There is only one thing left ... I am resolved
To die, if he must die, in the same swift hour.
Can any woman lose the precious name
Of virtue in which she trusted, and still live
Branded with shame?

CHORUS: All hope must not be lost
Before the event, although the thing you dread
May well be terrible.

DEIANEIRA: Hope? What kind of hope
Can proffer any comfort, when contrivance
Has overrun discretion?

CHORUS: Yet anger mellows
In the presence of innocent fault, as it will for you.

DEIANEIRA: So let the innocent think; the blemished heart
Knows better.

CHORUS: Silence is now the wisest course –
Unless you wish to tell your son. Hyllus,
The one who went to find his father, is here.

Enter HYLLUS.

HYLLUS: O mother, I could wish you were dead ... that
    you were not my mother ...
That you could be changed into someone other and better
Than what you are ...
I could wish that any one of these things were true.

DEIANEIRA: My son, how have I given you cause to hate me?

HYLLUS: Do you know that today you have killed your
    husband, my father?

DEIANEIRA: Hyllus! What are you saying?

HYLLUS: Nothing but the truth.

No one can undo what has been seen to happen.

DEIANEIRA: What do you mean?

Who is your witness to this thing you charge me with?

HYLLUS: No other witness but my own eyes.

I saw my father's terrible sufferings.

DEIANEIRA: You found him? Were with him at the time?
Where was it?

HYLLUS: Do you want to know? Then let me tell you.

The noble city of Eurytus was taken and destroyed, and
my father went on his way loaded with trophies and the
loot of victory, till he came to Cenaeum, the long sea-cape
of Euboea. Here he dedicated in a wooded precinct an
altar to Zeus his father; and it was here, to my great joy,
that I first set eyes on him. He was on the point of cele-
brating a sacrificial feast of special splendour, when Lichas,
his personal envoy, arrived from home, bringing your fatal
offering, the robe. He put it on as you desired, and pro-
ceeded with the sacrifice. Twelve oxen were slain, chosen
for their unblemished excellence as the first of the spoil.
After them followed other victims of every kind, a hundred
in all; and my poor father recited the prayers, serene and
happy with the fine apparel on him.

As the flame of the sacrifice began to feed on the blood
and on the juice of the pinewood, a sweat broke out upon
his skin, and the tunic was seen to cling tightly to every
inch of his body, as if moulded to his form by the hand of a
modeller; pain racked and gnawed at his bones; and a poison
like that of some vicious deadly serpent began to consume
him. He shouted for Lichas – poor man, as if he was to blame
for your wickedness – accusing him of a treacherous plot
in bringing him the garment; and he, knowing nothing of
the truth, answered, to his cost, that the gift was from your

hands alone, and that he had delivered it as he received it from you. When my father heard this, a spasm of agony wrenched his lungs, and he seized the man by the joint of his ankle and dashed him upon a rock rising out of the sea-foam. His skull was broken into fragments, and the hair was matted with the white marrow of the brain and with the blood.

My father's frenzy and the fate of his herald set the people moaning with grief and awe; but no one dared to confront him. Flung to the ground or leaping into the air, he filled all the cliffs and headlands of Locris and the Euboean shores with the echo of his piercing cries. And so, tossing and crying out till his strength was spent, execrating his fatal union with a miscreant and his alliance with the house of Oineus, which had brought him to destruction, at last through the enveloping smoke he turned his searching eyes on me, as I stood in the great throng, weeping; and when he saw me he called to me and said: 'My son, come here to me; do not hide from my misery; even if you must catch death from me, come. Carry me away, and lay me where I shall be seen no more; that would be best; or if that be too hard a thing for your pity, take me quickly to some other land. I must not die here'.

In obedience to this command, we laid him in the hold of a ship, and rowed him over to this shore – a pitiful task, as he lay there moaning in torment. Whether he is still alive or not, I do not know – but you will see him presently. This is what you have done, mother, to my father; Done it deliberately; and your guilt is known. May avenging Justice and the Furies punish you! This – God forgive me – is my solemn prayer. And it is forgiven, for it is you that have absolved me, When you killed the greatest man in all the world, Whose equal you will never see.

DEIANEIRA *goes silently towards the house.*

CHORUS: Deianeira? Have you nothing to say before you go?
  Will not your silence plead as loud as words
  On your accuser's side?
HYLLUS: But let her go.
  And luck be with her, wheresoever she goes,
  So long as it is from my sight. My mother ...
  What right has she to that respected title,
  Whose actions could be so unmotherly?
  Goodbye to her; and may she be as happy
  As she has made my father.

> DEIANEIRA *goes in;* HYLLUS *leaves the stage*
> *by another way.*

CHORUS:
  It is here, sisters – the moment has come and the word that
     was spoken
  So long ago is with us now; the voice of heaven
  Spoke, and foretold that the twelfth month of the twelfth
     year
  Would bring to the son of Zeus the end of all his labours.
  Now it comes home, like a ship sped safe and sound to its
     haven –
  Surely when a man is dead his days of slavery are over.
  How shall we hope that Heracles will see another day,
  Already wrapped in the mist of death, smeared with the
     poison,
  The death-spawn hatched in the womb of the fiery serpent,
     the Centaur's
  Mortal device clinging to his flesh, the ghost of the Hydra
  Clinging, and all the arrows of the black-haired lying monster
  Stinging his flesh with sharpest pangs of unimaginable tor-
     ment.

  Poor lady, she had not foreseen
  This tragedy, she only knew

There was harm to come, with a second wife
Brought into her house, and what she did
She did deliberately; the consequence
Was not her doing – a deadly plot
Contrived in an accidental meeting.
For this her heart must break,
For this her eyes must shed
Their tender rain. And we shall see,
In what is yet to come, the consummation
Of deepest villainy.

The river of tears has burst its banks.
O pity our master, suffering
Such torments as no enemy
Had ever put on him. O where
Is now the spear of victory,
The gleaming steel that won a bride
And ravished her away
From high Oechalia?
Ah but we know whose handiwork
Is here; it is the Cyprian goddess,
The silent minister of these events.

> *They break off, their attention arrested by sounds from
> within. Then severally:*

CHORUS: Is it my fancy, or was that a cry of grief
That came from the house just then?

> (*The* NURSE *is heard weeping within.*)

– Yes, there again. There's no mistaking the sound.
It is someone in trouble. What can have happened now?
– O look, the nurse is coming to tell us something.
And, poor old lady, how distressed she looks!

> *Enter the* NURSE.

NURSE: I knew there was nothing but a heap of trouble,
To come of that thing that was sent to Heracles.

CHORUS: O Nurse, what has happened?

NURSE: Deianeira is gone,
Gone her last journey, without setting foot out of doors.

CHORUS: Not dead?

NURSE: Ay, that's the whole story.

CHORUS: Deianeira dead?

NURSE: Yes, she is dead.

CHORUS: O poor doomed soul! How did she die?

NURSE: It was an awful deed.

CHORUS: What deed ... so swiftly done?

NURSE: Took her own life.

CHORUS: In rage ... in madness? What sharp passion
Edged the weapon?
This second death ...
How could she do it all alone?

NURSE: A sword, one fatal stroke –

CHORUS: And you were there, woman,
And saw the outrage!

NURSE: I saw, I was there beside her.

CHORUS: What was it? How did she do it? O speak!

NURSE: All her own doing ... no hand but hers.

CHORUS: Is it possible?

NURSE: 'Tis true.

CHORUS: This is the heir
Born to the newly wed!
Vengeance and death
Born in the house!

NURSE: Vengeance indeed: if you had been there to see
All that she did, you would have wept still more.

CHORUS:
And could one woman's hand do so much mischief?

NURSE: Indeed it could; as you shall hear; then say
If I speak truth or not.
As you saw, she came back into the house alone.

Her son was in the courtyard, making ready
To take a stretcher-bed to meet his father;
She saw him, but hid herself from everyone.
Then she knelt down before the household altars
And cried out loud that they would soon be left
With no-one else to visit them. Up and down,
All through the house she went, weeping, poor lady,
As she touched each thing she had been wont to use;
Weeping again, each time she saw the face
Of one of her servants, for she loved them all;
Crying for her own woes, and for the emptiness
Of the house that no more sons of hers would see.
Then she was silent, and hurried quickly away
To the room she had shared with Heracles. I watched,
Spying from a secret place. She took out bedclothes
And spread them out upon her husband's bed;
And then she threw herself upon it, and sat
Crouched in the middle of the bed, breaking her heart
In torrents of hot tears. 'Goodbye,' she cried,
'My happy bride-bed – bed of blissful sleep,
All ended now – this is goodbye for ever!'
Then, silent again, she grasped the golden buckle
Above her breast, loosed it with trembling hands
And stripped her left arm bare, and all the side
Nearest her heart. I ran as fast as I could
To tell her son what she was thinking of.
In the time it took to fetch him – it was done;
And there we found her, with the two-edged sword
Thrust through the stomach to her heart. Her son
Cried bitterly at what he saw; he knew,
Poor lad, it was his anger drove her to it.
By now he had learnt, too late, from others here
That what she had done was all a mistake – that spell
The Centaur taught her. So the unhappy boy

Wept bitterly, and could never make an end
Of crying over her, clinging to her lips,
Falling beside her, with his heart on hers.
'My wicked slander killed you!' – so he cried –
'And I shall lose my father and my mother
Both in this hour, and see them never again!'
So there it is. Only a foolish man
Would reckon on the future – one day, two,
Or more to come. Tomorrow – what is tomorrow?
'Tis nothing, until today is safely past.

CHORUS:

Two deaths, two sorrows, O
Where shall we weep?
Which is the heavier to bear,
This one or that, how can we know?

This here before our eyes,
That yet to come,
Yet to be seen; to see, to wait,
Are they not equal agonies?

Wind, sweep us away,
Sweep through this house with cleansing breath
And carry us to some other land,
Or we must die a death
Of instant terror, to see
Our God-born hero brought, they say,
Home on a bed of pain
Past remedy –
Horror that none can understand,
Unspeakable and strange.

It is nearer now, it is here,
As we cry like birds of sorrow. Now
There are feet of strangers on the way . . .

Yes, they are bringing him – how?
The voices are hushed, and slow
The feet of those that carry a dear
Burden in silence. Ah,
Why do they so?
Is he alive? O say,
Is he dead or sleeping?

HERACLES *is carried in on a litter, with an* ELDER *in attendance,* HYLLUS *following.*

HYLLUS: Alas, alas, my father! Alas, I am lost, alone without you. Alas, my father!

ELDER: Do not cry out, my boy; you will only provoke his suffering and kindle his wrath afresh. He is in a swoon, but still alive. Keep a hold on your lips . . .

HYLLUS: Is he alive, sir?

ELDER: He is asleep, I tell you; do not wake him or you will revive his pain, which comes and goes fitfully.

HYLLUS: How shall I bear this heavy blow? O my heart breaks!

HERACLES (*awaking*): O God, O God!
Where am I? Who are these
Watching me on this rack
Of endless agony? . . .
O misery! Again
The tooth bites . . . Ah, the monster –

ELDER (*to* HYLLUS):
Did I not tell you it would be better to be silent
Instead of chasing the sleep from his eyes and brain?

HYLLUS: I could not bear so pitiful a sight.

HERACLES: Was it for this, O God,
Was it for this reward
I made my offerings
Upon the altar-stones

Of Cenaeum? To be so damned –
Would I had never seen
That death-trap, where I found
This exquisite perfection
Of maddening pain,
Never to be allayed.
What balm is there, what medicine,
What far-fetched miracle
Could ever cure this plague –
Save Zeus alone?

(*The* ELDER *ministers to him*).

Ah, leave me, leave me to my last sleep;
Leave me to my end, my rest . . .
What are you doing? You only wake
The slumbering pain . . .
Ah, there it comes again to devour me . . .
What men are you, you falsest, meanest of all the Greeks?
I wore myself to death for you, toiling through forests and
    seas
To root out evil, and where is there one of you brave enough
To end my sufferings with merciful fire or sword?
O who will come and strike
The head from this hideous body of pain? O! . . .

ELDER: Help me, son, this is more than I can do alone.
You are stronger and better able than I to comfort him.

HYLLUS:
My arms are round him: but there is nothing more that I
Or anyone can do to make him live again
Released from suffering. This visitation is from God.

HERACLES: Where are you, my son?
Hold me, here . . . here . . . and lift me up . . .
O God!
The foul fiend grips me again . . .
He will have my life –

There is no help against him.
O Pallas, Pallas, I am in torment! O my son,
For pity's sake, your sword – strike, in just mercy strike
Over my heart, here, and put an end to the pain
That galls my flesh. And let me see the same swift death
Punish your mother for this impious thing she has done.
Sweet Death, brother of God, send me to sleep, to sleep,
And end this misery in one sharp stroke of doom.
CHORUS: O women – to hear our master in such torment!
So great a man driven by so much pain!
HERACLES: This is the worst of all the famous burdens
This body has shouldered, all the hot encounters
These hands have fought in; none was ever like it.
The wife of Zeus – the tyrannous Eurystheus –
None of them laid such heavy pains upon me
As that false-smiling woman, Oineus' daughter,
Who wrapped me in this garment of damnation,
This net to strangle me. Stuck fast upon me
It has devoured my vitals, inch by inch,
Sucked out the channels of my breath, and drunk
My living blood – a man without a body,
Imprisoned in a death that has no name!
No warrior's spear, no army of earth-born Giants,
No savage beast, no Greek, no alien tongue,
No land of all that I have fought to cleanse,
Did such a thing to me. One woman,
Unmanly woman, unarmed, has vanquished me.

   My son, now show me that you are my son,
And never say you hold the name of mother
Higher than mine. Bring her out here to me!
Bring out your mother with your own hands, here,
And give her into mine! And when you see us
Both suffering side by side – my body in torment,
Hers flayed with the punishment that is her due –

Say which is the prettier sight. Go, son! You must . . .
O pity me, son, whom all the world will pity,
Brought down to this: moaning and crying aloud
Like any girl – a thing no man alive
Has ever seen me do before; no pain,
In all my journeys into suffering,
Has ever wrung a murmur from my lips.
And now I am proved no better than a woman . . .

　　Come nearer; stand beside me, son, and look,
Look at my agony . . . Throw off these coverings! . . .
Look at this wretched corpse! Look, all of you,
At my condition! . . .
Ah! There it is again . . .
That scorching flame,
Hot arrows piercing through my sides! . . .
The fight is not yet over, then. The monster
Will have more blood of me . . .
O King of Death, receive me!
Strike me, O Fire of God!
Lord! Father! Fling down a thunderbolt
Upon my head! . . .
Still it devours me,
Again it comes at me
With ever-increasing power . . .

　　O hands, hands, shoulders, breast, and arms, dear arms!
Do you remember the lion of Nemea,
At whom the shepherds quaked – that savage beast
Whom no man else had ever come to terms with –
It was you that fought and killed him. Do you remember
The Hydra of Lerna – and those abominable
Monstrous man-horses, a rude and violent breed
Intractable to any human ruling –
The Erymanthian boar – the invincible
Three-headed hound of Hell, the whelp of Echidna –

The dragon-warder of the golden fruit
In the far-west land – you fought and beat them all.
Ay, and from other battles, tens of thousands,
In which I played a part, not one man, none,
Carried his trophy home to tell a tale
Of victory over me. And here I lie,
Demolished, dismembered, mangled into rags
By heaven knows what bedevilment . . .
They say my mother was a noble lady;
They say my father was the King of Heaven.
Whatever I am – and even as I am –
A thing that cannot crawl, a piece of nothing –
You shall know this : I've something yet to do
With her that worked this mischief. Let her come out!
I'll show her a way to let the whole world know
I lived to punish evil-doers, and died
Doing the same.

CHORUS: O Hellas, sorrow, sorrow
I see before you, if he must die.

HYLLUS: My father,
Now that your silence gives me leave to speak,
Hear me. However great your torment, listen
To what I have a right to ask; and listen
With less of that impatient rage that pricks you.
You don't know what you are asking; this revenge
You have set your heart on, is not possible;
Nor have you cause for anger.

HERACLES: Say what you will.
I am too ill to understand your preaching.

HYLLUS: My mother . . . I want to tell you where she is,
And that she never meant to harm you.

HERACLES: Traitor!
You dare to speak her name to me – that mother
Who killed your father!

HYLLUS: I must speak of her,
  As she is now.
HERACLES: Speak of her as she was –
  A miscreant.
HYLLUS: No – as she is today
  I speak of her – and you must know the truth
  And own it.
HERACLES: Speak; and betray me at your peril.
HYLLUS: This is the truth. We have just found her dead.
HERACLES: Who dared to kill her? This is a revelation
  As black as it is wonderful.
HYLLUS: She died
  By her own hand; no other was there to do it.
HERACLES: She should have died by mine. O miserable!
HYLLUS:
  There is more that you must hear, and when you hear
  You will resign your anger.
HERACLES: Impossible.
  What is it you have to say?
HYLLUS: It was all a mistake.
  She did wrong, trying to do you good.
HERACLES: Good, villain?
  Was it good to kill your father?
HYLLUS: This is what happened:
  She thought to work upon you with a love-charm,
  Seeing this woman whom you meant to marry;
  But all went wrong –
HERACLES: A love-charm? Who in Trachis
  Deals in such potent medicines?
HYLLUS: Nessus the Centaur
  Prompted her long ago to use some spell
  To kindle your affections.
HERACLES: Nessus the Centaur! ...
  O Death, Death!

This is the end. There is no more light for me,
But utter darkness. Now I know the truth . . .
Go, boy – my hour has come – go quickly, son –
Bring all your brothers here, and bring Alcmena
My mother, who was loved, unhappily,
By Zeus; and you shall hear, before I die,
What certain oracles have told me. Go.

HYLLUS: They are not here. Your mother has made her home
 At Tiryns, by the sea; the others, we are told,
 Are in the city of Thebes. We who are here
 Will do whatever must be done for you.

HERACLES: Then listen. The time has come for you to show
 What sort of stuff my son is made of.
 Some time ago it was revealed to me
 By my great Father, that I could never be killed
 By any living creature, only by one
 That had passed the border between life and death.
 And so it is, as the oracle foretold;
 Death comes to the living from the dead; the Centaur
 Kills Heracles. And more – this ancient prophecy
 Agrees with what was afterwards revealed.
 Listen: I heard it from the talking oak
 That speaks my Father's word, and wrote it down
 In the grove of the Selli, the sleepers on the mountains.
 Thus said the Word; that in this very hour
 Which now lives with us, the end should be accomplished
 Of all the labours that have been laid upon me . . .
 The end of toil, I thought, should be the beginning
 Of happiness; but what it meant was – death.
 The dead rest from their labours.
 Now, my son,
 Since all is patently to be fulfilled,
 I need your help. Do not provoke my wrath
 By any denial. Consent, and help me, son,

Knowing, as well you must, that best commandment -
Obey your father.

HYLLUS: I am afraid to think
What your next word will be; but I consent.

HERACLES: First, give me your hand.

HYLLUS: What is this promise for?

HERACLES: Give me your hand! No disobedience!

HYLLUS: There, then ... As you wish.

HERACLES: Swear by the head of Zeus,
The father that begat me.

HYLLUS: What must I swear?

HERACLES: Swear faithfully to perform
The task I give you.

HYLLUS: I swear it, Zeus be my witness.

HERACLES: On pain of tribulation, if you depart from it.

HYLLUS: There will be no tribulation, and no departing from it.
So be it as you say.

HERACLES: So be it ... Now,
You know the summit of the sacred mountain,
Oeta, the mount of Zeus?

HYLLUS: I know the place,
The hill-top altar where I have often stood.

HERACLES: You are to carry me up there, yourself
With any other helpers you may choose.
When you get there, cut down a pile of branches
Of firm-set oak and the robust wild-olive,
Then lay my body on the pyre, and kindle it
With a flaming torch of pine. Do this in silence -
I will have no weeping there, no lamentations -
If you are truly a son of mine. Fail me,
And you shall have my curse upon your head,
Even from the grave, for ever.

HYLLUS: O my father,
What sort of task is this to put upon me?

HERACLES: It is what must be done. Refuse,
And be the son of some man else, not mine!

HYLLUS: It is too much. How can you ask me, father,
To take your life – your blood upon my hands?

HERACLES: I do not ask it. I make you my physician:
Your act alone shall cure me of my sickness.

HYLLUS: How? Heal your body by setting fire to it?

HERACLES: Does that thought frighten you? Well, do the rest.

HYLLUS: I cannot refuse to carry you to the place.

HERACLES: And build the pyre, as I instructed you?

HYLLUS: So long as I need lay no finger on it,
I will see it built; I give my word for that.

HERACLES: Well, that will be enough. One small thing more
To add to these much greater services –

HYLLUS: However great, it shall be done.

HERACLES: You have heard
Of the girl, the daughter of Eurytus?

HYLLUS: Iole?

HERACLES: You know then. This is what I want you to do.
After my death, as you revere the oath
You have sworn to your father, make this girl your wife.
Do this for your father. No other man but you
Must take her, since she has been mine
And lain beside me. Marry her, my son;
I beg you. You have been faithful in so much,
To refuse a little thing would cancel out
My former gratitude.

HYLLUS: What can I say?
I must not cross you in your agony.
But this last fancy that possesses you –
It is intolerable.

HERACLES: What are you saying?
You mean to disobey me?

HYLLUS: Who could do it?

That woman – the sole cause of my mother's death,
Of your condition too – take her to wife?
No man could do it, unless the avenging fiends
Had driven him from his wits. I'd rather die
Than mate with my worst enemy.

HERACLES: Defy me,
Will you? Defy me in the hour of death?
The vengeance of the gods will punish you
For disobedience!

HYLLUS: Father, I fear
Your sickened rage will have no bounds.

HERACLES: 'Tis you
Provoke my sleeping pain!

HYLLUS: What shall I do?
I am helpless every way I turn.

HERACLES: And will be,
As long as you refuse to obey your father.

HYLLUS: Must I consent to such an impious act?

HERACLES: To grant my heart's desire is no impiety.

HYLLUS: It is your order – and my sacred duty?

HERACLES: It is – the gods be witness!

HYLLUS: I will do it.
The gods be witness that it is your doing;
It cannot be sin to obey my father's charge.

HERACLES:
That's my good son, at last ... Now, lose no time
But make your promise good.
Take me to the pyre
And lay me on it, before new torments come
To bite and rend me.
Lift me up; make haste;
This is my rest at last, my end of troubles ...
The end of Heracles.

HYLLUS: Father, your wish

Is our commandment, and we must obey.

HERACLES: At once, then, while the pain still sleeps . . .

(Four of the attendants prepare to lift the litter.)

O patience, muzzle my lips
With iron, lock them in stone,
Stifle the cry.
The way is hard, but the end
Is consolation.

HYLLUS: Lift . . .

(The cortège begins to move off.)

Let all men here forgive me,
And mark the malevolence
Of the unforgiving gods
In this event. We call them
Fathers of sons, and they
Look down unmoved
Upon our tragedies.

The future is hidden from us.
This is the present –
Our grief, who see it;
His untold agony,
Who must endure it;
And their reproach,
Who let it be.

Women of Trachis, you have leave to go.
You have seen strange things,
The awful hand of death, new shapes of woe,
Uncounted sufferings;
And all that you have seen
Is God.

EXEUNT

PHILOCTETES

Philoctetes the Malian, son of Poeas, had accompanied the Grecian expedition to Troy, but on visiting the temple of the goddess Chryse had been bitten in the foot by a venomous serpent, the guardian of the shrine. His noxious and incurable wound aroused so much revulsion among his former comrades that they banished him to the uninhabited island of Lemnos, where he eked out a wretched existence throughout the ten years of the Trojan war. At length it was revealed to the Greek leaders that Troy could only be taken by the help of the invincible bow and arrows of Heracles, and these were in the possession of Philoctetes, having been given to him by Heracles at his death.

Odysseus and Neoptolemus, son of Achilles, are sent to recall Philoctetes from his exile and bring him with the bow and arrows to Troy. But Philoctetes is unwilling to make peace with those who treated him so cruelly, and only by the intervention of the deified Heracles is he persuaded to return and help the Greeks to victory.

PHILOCTETES

*

CHARACTERS

Odysseus
Neoptolemus
Philoctetes
Heracles
A Sailor
Chorus of Sailors

*

*The scene represents a desolate part of the coast of Lemnos. A rocky
path leads upwards to the half-hidden entrance to a cave.*
Enter ODYSSEUS *and* NEOPTOLEMUS, *with a*
SAILOR *following.*

ODYSSEUS: This is the coast of Lemnos, a desolate island
  In the midst of the sea, where no man walks or lives.
  Now, young Neoptolemus, son of the great Achilles,
  This is the place where, many years ago,
  Acting on the orders of our overlords,
  I left Philoctetes the Malian, Poeas' son,
  Lamed by a festering ulcer in his foot,
  At which he would moan and howl incessantly;
  Our camp was never free of his frantic wailing –
  Never a moment's pause for libation or prayer,
  But the silence was desecrated by his tortured cries.
  The story's a long one; I cannot tell it now.
  If he once finds out I'm here, my clever device
  To capture him will fall to the ground. To work!
  I need your help.
  First, see if you can find

A cave with a double entrance, the sort of place
To afford two sun-traps on a chilly day
Or a cool retreat for sleep in the height of summer,
Fanned by a current of air. A little below,
To the left, there should be a spring of running water,
Unless it's now dried up. Go quietly,
And see if there's any sign of the fellow still
In his old accustomed haunts; and bring me word;
And then I'll tell you what we've got to do,
And we'll go to work together.

NEOPTOLEMUS *climbs the rock.*

NEOPTOLEMUS: Odysseus, sir!
We haven't far to look. There *is* a cave,
Just as you say.

ODYSSEUS: Above you or below?
I cannot see from here.

NEOPTOLEMUS: It's rather high.
I hear no sign of anyone moving about.

ODYSSEUS: Perhaps he's asleep inside. Look in and see.

NEOPTOLEMUS: The place seems empty; not a man in sight.

ODYSSEUS: Is there any sign of human habitation?

NEOPTOLEMUS: There's a pile of leaves pressed down, as if
someone had slept on it.

ODYSSEUS: And nothing else? Is the rest of the chamber
empty?

NEOPTOLEMUS: There's a rough wooden cup, some clumsy
person's handiwork
By the look of it. And here's some tinder-wood.

ODYSSEUS: That sounds like the fellow's goods and chattels.

NEOPTOLEMUS: Hullo!
Here's something else: rags hanging out to dry,
Stained, it appears, with the flux of a nasty wound.

ODYSSEUS: The man is here all right, no doubt about it.
This is his home; he can't be far away;

How could he be, crippled with that old sore?
He'll be out hunting for his dinner, or for some herb
He's discovered to soothe his pain.

        (*Calling to* NEOPTOLEMUS)

Send your man
To scout around. I mustn't be caught by surprise;
He'd rather catch me than any Greek alive.

NEOPTOLEMUS: I will (*he sends the Sailor out of sight*).
He's going to keep an eye on the path.

        (*Coming down to join* ODYSSEUS)

Now, what's the next move?

ODYSSEUS: Listen, son of Achilles:
You've come on a mission that calls for all your strength –
Not only bodily strength. If you are surprised
At anything I say, remember you are here to help me.

NEOPTOLEMUS: What do you want me to do?

ODYSSEUS: To *trick* Philoctetes
By a tale you must tell him. When he asks you who you are
And where you come from, say you're the son of Achilles –
No need for a lie so far. You're homeward bound,
Tell him, and have left the Greek invading force
With a mighty grudge against them; they begged and
    prayed you
To come from home, as if the capture of Troy
Depended on you alone; and when you came
And asked for your father's arms, as was your right,
Refused to give them, and gave them instead to
    Odysseus . . .
Oh yes, you may call me any names you like,
The viler the better – I shan't mind – but remember,
If you fail us now, the wrath of all the Greeks
Will be on your head. You've got to get that bow
From Philoctetes, or never capture Troy.
And listen –

Here is the reason why you can approach him
Rather than I, without arousing suspicion.
You made this voyage of your own accord, not bound
By oath to anyone, under no compulsion,
Having taken no part in the original expedition.
I have no such excuse. If he catches sight of me
While he still holds the bow, it means my death,
And yours as well. No; this is our only chance.
The weapon is irresistible, and we must plan
A stratagem to steal it.
　　　　　　Of course, my boy,
I know it goes against the grain with you
To lie, or act deceitfully; but then,
Success is worth an effort, make it now.
We shall be justified in the end; for the present
Let honesty go hang, only for a day,
I beg you; and then you can live for ever after
A paragon of virtue. Will you do it?

NEOPTOLEMUS:

I confess, sir, there are things that offend my conscience
Even in hearing, and therefore still more in action.
Deceit is not my nature; nor, I am told,
Was it my father's. I'd rather beat this man
By force than by deception. In any case,
One against many, and with only one sound foot,
He isn't likely to get the better of us.
I know I've been sent to help you in this mission.
And I'd hate to fail you now; but really, sir,
I'd rather lose by fair means than win by foul.

ODYSSEUS:

My lad, you're your father's son. When I was your age,
My hand was readier than my tongue; but now
I've learnt by much and bitter experience
Words count for more than deeds in the world of men.

NEOPTOLEMUS:

Have you any orders for me, other than to tell a lie?

ODYSSEUS: Just to use a little deception to entrap Philoctetes.

NEOPTOLEMUS:

Is it necessary? Might not persuasion be sufficient?

ODYSSEUS:

You will never persuade him, still less take him by force.

NEOPTOLEMUS:

Why, has he such terrible strength at his command?

ODYSSEUS: Arrows that never miss, flying to kill.

NEOPTOLEMUS:

I see: so it's dangerous even to approach the man?

ODYSSEUS: It is; unless, as I say, you use some stratagem.

NEOPTOLEMUS:

Don't you believe it wrong to tell a lie, sir?

ODYSSEUS: No, if success and safety depend upon it.

NEOPTOLEMUS:

I don't know if I could do it; my face would betray me.

ODYSSEUS:

It's for your own good; you can't afford to be squeamish.

NEOPTOLEMUS:

What good will it do me for him to come to Troy?

ODYSSEUS: Without those arrows Troy will never be ours.

NEOPTOLEMUS:

I thought it was I that was to win that victory.

ODYSSEUS: You and the arrows: neither without the other.

NEOPTOLEMUS:

In that case, there's nothing for it; we must make them ours.

ODYSSEUS: Two prizes await you when you've done the deed.

NEOPTOLEMUS: What? Tell me, and I might do it.

ODYSSEUS: A prize for intelligence,

And a prize for courage.

NEOPTOLEMUS: Say no more. I'll do it,

And conscience can be hanged!

ODYSSEUS: Good. You remember
What I advised you to do?

NEOPTOLEMUS: I know. I'll do it,
Now I've made up my mind.

ODYSSEUS: Wait for him here.
I'll keep away, not to be seen with you;
And I'll send our watcher back to the ship. Later,
If you seem to be taking longer than I expect,
I'll send the fellow out again, disguised
(To aid the deception) as a merchant skipper.
He'll spin some suitable yarn, so you watch out
And take your cue from him. Now I'll be off,
And leave the rest to you. May we be guided
By Hermes the subtle, the finder of ways, and victory,
And Athena Polias, always at my side!

Exit.

Enter the CHORUS *of sailors from*
NEOPTOLEMUS' *ship.*

CHORUS: Captain, this is a strange
And lonely piece of land.
What are the orders, sir?
'Tis a canny creature, I reckon,
We've come to meet.
Do we tell him all, or no?

'Tis the power of God Almighty
Quickens the wits of a man,
As it has in you, lad, filled
With power and strength sent down
From eternal ages.

Give us our orders, sir.

NEOPTOLEMUS: First, you will want to see for yourselves
The place he lives in, here by the shore.

Look, there it is. There's nothing to fear.
The monster's not at home at present.
He's out for a walk. When he returns,
Come forward carefully. Watch my signals,
And be ready to give me any assistance.

CHORUS: Trust us for that, Captain.
We'll keep an eye on you,
As we always do.

      (NEOPTOLEMUS *climbs up to the cave.*)

What sort of a place has he got
To make a home in here?
And – which is more important –
Where is he now, I wonder?
He might spring suddenly on us
If we don't know where he is hiding,
Whether he's gone away, or
Is biding his time somewhere
Inside or out.

NEOPTOLEMUS: Look, here's his house, this crib in the rock.
Front door, back door –

CHORUS: Where can he be?
Poor devil.

NEOPTOLEMUS: He cannot be far away.
He'll have hobbled off to look for food.
They say that's how he lives, poor creature,
Painfully hunting with bow and arrows,
And no one to help him cure his trouble.

CHORUS: 'Tis a pitiful life for a man,
And no mistake. Lonesome.
Not a living soul to talk to;
No one to help him bear his pains;
Pitiful. Suffering like that.
Pretty near out of his mind,
I should say, with all he has to put up with.

You'd wonder a man could stand it.
To think the gods could send
Such mischief to man!
'Tis ever a curse for a man to be marked
Above the common lot.
Son of a high-born house,
Likely as not, as good as the best;
And now, lost and alone
With the furred and feathered creatures,
Tortured with want and the pain
He can never cure;
And none to answer his cries
But the echo in far-off hills.

NEOPTOLEMUS: I know his story. It is not strange.
I think it is under the will of heaven
He suffers, and by the anger of Chryse.
His torments now, and his loneliness,
Are the work of a god; he has those arrows
Holy and invincible, and must not use them
On Trojan soil, till the due time comes
When they are to compass the city's fall.

CHORUS: Hark! What was that?

NEOPTOLEMUS: What now?

CHORUS: A sound like the weary cry
Of a man in pain.
Was it there? No, there.
I can hear it again.
A dragging step, surely, and the voice
Of a suffering creature,
As plain as plain.
Come, sir –

NEOPTOLEMUS: What shall we do?

CHORUS: Look alive, the man is near.
And that's no ditty or shepherd-song

He sings, but the desperate moan
Of a stumbling wounded castaway
Looking out on an empty sea.

Enter PHILOCTETES, *a pitiful figure in ragged garments, the
famous bow in his hand, and his wounded foot swathed in crude
bandages.*

PHILOCTETES: Ahoy there! ...
Men, who are you? What country is it you come from
To this strange coast? There is no harbour here,
No home for any man ... What blood? What city?
I cannot guess. Greeks surely, though, I'd say,
By the look of your clothes – and God be thanked for that.
If I could hear your language ... Have no fear!
You're scared at my looks, more like a savage creature
Than a man. But have no fear; pity me rather.
I am a poor lonely creature, a castaway
Without a friend in the world, much wronged ...
Speak, men!
Speak, if you come as friends. Answer, O answer!
We must not part without a word.

NEOPTOLEMUS: My friend,
We are Greeks. That question can be answered first.

PHILOCTETES: O lovely sound! After so many years
To hear that greeting! O my lad, my son,
What brings you here? What errand? What blessed wind?
Who are you? Tell me. Let me hear you speak.

NEOPTOLEMUS: The island of Scyros is my homeland. Home
Is where I am bound for now. My name, Neoptolemus,
Son of Achilles. There you have it all.

PHILOCTETES: Achilles' son! I knew him. He was my friend.
And Scyros – lovely country! You, his child:
Old Lycomedes was your foster-father.
How come you to this coast, then? And from where?

NEOPTOLEMUS: From Troy, this voyage.

PHILOCTETES: Troy? But how is that?
  You were not with us when we sailed there first.

NEOPTOLEMUS:
  'We'? What, were you one of that gallant band?

PHILOCTETES: O lad, can it be you don't know whom
    you're talking to?

NEOPTOLEMUS: Someone I've never seen before, surely.

PHILOCTETES: You never heard my name? You never heard
  Anything of the calamity that has kept me here
  More dead than alive?

NEOPTOLEMUS: Nothing at all, I assure you.

PHILOCTETES: O my misery! How the gods must hate me!
  Left in this plight, and never a word of it
  Brought to my home or to any corner of Greece.
  They enjoy their joke in silence, who infamously
  Cast me away; while here my old infirmity
  Thrives undiminished, ever-increasing. Son,
  Son of Achilles, you know me, you must have heard
  Of the man who was master of the weapons of Heracles,
  Poeas' son, Philoctetes. I am he,
  Whom our two captains, with the Cephallenian,
  Marooned here by a devilish trick; helpless
  They left me, wasting with a deadly wound,
  A venomous serpent's bite, searing my flesh;
  Left me with it alone, lad; cast me ashore
  And went upon their way. It was when their fleet
  Was sailing from Chryse and chanced to put in here.
  And thankful they must have been to see me sleeping
  – We'd had a stormy passage – in the lee of a rock
  On shore, where they left me and went, giving me nothing
  But a handful of beggarly rags and a morsel of food.
  May heaven serve them the like!
    Think what I felt, lad,
  Waking to find them gone; what an awakening!

O, how I wept and cursed my fate! Imagine
How I felt when I saw that every ship was gone
Of those I sailed with, not a man on the island,
Not one to befriend me or lend me a helping hand
In the trouble that racked me. Whichever way I looked,
There was nothing, nothing beside me but misery,
And that in abundance, lad.

 So time and time went on, and all alone
Here in this little crib, day after day,
I had to manage as best I might. This bow
Was servant to my belly; many a bird
It has brought to the ground; and mind you, every time
I killed with an arrow from this string, it was I
That had to crawl and drag myself along,
With this wretched foot, to where the quarry fell.
And then for water, or wood to burn – the frost
Is sharp in winter – out I had to go
In search of it. I would have had no fire,
But that I managed to coax its secret out
Laboriously rubbing stone on stone.
And so I kept alive. Roof and a fire:
What more could I want? – save healing of my pain.

 But now to tell you of the island, lad.
'Tis a place no man afloat would choose to run to;
Here is no anchorage, much less port or market
For a man of business, nothing at all to give
A visitor welcome. No man in his senses
Makes this a port of call. Now and again
Some accident would bring a man this way –
Such things must happen in a lifetime – well,
What do my visitors do? Talk kindly to me,
Give me a little charity, food maybe,
Or bits of clothing, but, if I mention it,
A passage home – no; anything but that.

Ten years a-dying of hunger and wretchedness,
To keep alive this glutton pain!

(*A spasm of agony.*)

The hand of Odysseus, the hands of the sons of Atreus
Did this to me, boy. May the gods of heaven
Pay them in full with sufferings like mine!

CHORUS: Truly we are as sorry for you, son of Poeas,
As any that ever came to visit you.

NEOPTOLEMUS: Indeed, yes; I myself can testify
You speak the truth, for I have suffered too
At the hands of the sons of Atreus, and the hand of Odysseus.

PHILOCTETES: You too? Have you a cause for indignation,
A score against those villains?

NEOPTOLEMUS: That I have,
And long for the day when I shall pay it off
And let Mycenae know, and Sparta know
That Scyros is the mother of brave sons.

PHILOCTETES:
Bravo, lad! Well then, tell us, what is the reason,
This mighty grudge you bear against them?

NEOPTOLEMUS: Sir,
I'll tell you as well as I can, though it won't be easy.
I came to Troy, and they insulted me.
The end appointed for my father's life –

PHILOCTETES: Achilles? The son of Peleus? No, not dead?
Tell me again, before anything else. Achilles?

NEOPTOLEMUS: Yes, dead; not killed by any mortal hand –
A god's. They say he fell to an arrow of Phoebus.

PHILOCTETES: Great victim of the great destroyer! O son,
Shall I ask more of you, or weep for him?

NEOPTOLEMUS: Sir, you have enough to suffer and to weep for;
You need not weep for others.

PHILOCTETES: That is true.
On with your tale, then. They insulted you?

NEOPTOLEMUS: This is the story. They came for me; the great Odysseus himself, and Phoenix, my father's former guardian, came in a ship with colours flying, to bring the message (whether true or false, I do not know) that, my father being dead, it was foretold that no one but I should accomplish the capture of Troy. Hearing this news, I lost no time in setting sail to return with them – chiefly for love of my dead father, and wishing to see him once before his burial. It was the only time I ever saw him. And there was glamour in their promise – the promise that I was to be the taker of the Trojan fortress.

Two days at sea, and wind and oar brought us to Sigeum, a land of sad memories for me. As I stepped ashore, the whole army gathered round me with joyful greetings; they could have sworn, they said, that the lost Achilles stood before them alive again. But he was dead. When I had mourned for him, I went, as soon as might be, to the sons of Atreus – my friends, as I supposed – and asked for my father's arms and all that had been his. And this, O God, this was their outrageous answer: 'Son of Achilles' they said, 'all that your father left behind him is yours to take, *except his weapons*; these we have already given to someone else – to Odysseus, the son of Laertes.' I sprang up with tears in my eyes, and bitter anger in my heart, and in my rage I said: 'How dare you make so bold as to give my arms to anyone but me, without my leave?' Odysseus himself was there. 'Young man' he said, 'they did quite right to give them to me; for as it happened it was I that saved them from capture, and their owner too.' I was so enraged, I called down every curse on him that I could think of – that *he* should rob me of my armour! At that, though not a choleric man as a rule, he angrily replied: 'When your place was here along with us, you chose to be elsewhere; and let me tell you this, boast as you will, you're mistaken

if you think you'll ever take those weapons back to Scyros.'
This was enough. Outraged, insulted, I sailed for home;
cheated and robbed by that scheming son of evil, Odysseus.
And yet I blame him less than those in command. As a state
depends on its leaders, so does an army; when men do
wrong, the teachers that have corrupted them are to blame.

    Well, that's the story. Heaven bless, as I do, every man
that hates the sons of Atreus!

CHORUS: Ay, by the Mother of All, Mother of Zeus himself,
  Goddess of Earth and Hills, Queen of the Mighty River
  Pactolus of the golden sands;
  It was to her we prayed that day
  When the sons of Atreus did this thing to him
  And took his father's arms away
  (Great Goddess, throned upon
  The Lion that devours the Bull!)
  To give Laertes' son
  A gift so wonderful!

PHILOCTETES: Sir, the credentials of your tale of injury
  Seem unmistakable; the very counterpart
  Of mine. I recognize the handiwork
  Of the brothers and Odysseus. He's a fellow
  With a ready tongue for any wicked speech
  Or mischief, to achieve his evil purposes.
  I know him well. There's nothing new in this.
  But what of Ajax the Great? I am surprised
  That he could bear to see such insult done.

NEOPTOLEMUS:
  Ah, he was gone, my friend. Had he been there,
  I should have had my rights.

PHILOCTETES: Ajax dead too?

NEOPTOLEMUS: Ay, gone into the darkness.

PHILOCTETES: O, the pity!
  And those two worthless ones – the spawn of Sisyphus

Bought by Laertes, and the son of Tydeus –
They will not die. They never should have lived.

NEOPTOLEMUS:
Not they. Make no mistake, they live and thrive,
High personages in the Grecian army.

PHILOCTETES: And is my good old friend, Nestor of Pylos,
Alive still? *He* could always find a way
To check their knavish tricks.

NEOPTOLEMUS: He is alive,
But in sad case, since he has lost his son
Whom he had with him, Antilochus.

PHILOCTETES: I'm sorry.
Two good men gone, whose loss comes nearer to me
Than any other. Well, well; what can we hope for
With these gone, and Odysseus still among us,
Whom we could well have spared?

NEOPTOLEMUS: The artful schemer!
But remember, Philoctetes, the cleverest rogue
Must meet his match some day, and bite the dust.

PHILOCTETES: But, heavens above, was not Patroclus there
To help you? He was your father's dearest friend.

NEOPTOLEMUS:
Dead too. Yes, that's the way of it, Philoctetes.
War never picks the worst men for his victims,
But always the best.

PHILOCTETES: I know it. And, by the by,
What of that worthless creature, shrewd of tongue
And cunning? What of him?

NEOPTOLEMUS: You mean Odysseus?

PHILOCTETES: No, no, not him. Thersites was his name;
One who would always be talking, and wouldn't be quiet
For anyone under the sun. Is he still living?

NEOPTOLEMUS:
I have heard that he is; though I didn't see him.

PHILOCTETES: He would be.
 Does nothing evil ever die? It seems
 A special providence protects all such.
 I think the gods delight to turn away
 All deep-dyed villains from the door of death
 And hale in all the good men. Why, then, why
 Praise we the gods, when, even while we praise,
 We find them evil?

NEOPTOLEMUS: For my part, from now on
 I shall steer clear of Troy and the sons of Atreus,
 And take good care never to choose my friends
 Where evil has the whip-hand over good
 And decent men are floored by cowards. Yes,
 From this time on I shall be satisfied
 With home and rocky Scyros. Now to my ship.
 Good-bye, and luck be with you, son of Poeas!
 I pray, as you do, that the blessed gods
 May soon relieve you of your suffering.
 We must be on our way, and ready to sail
 Whenever heaven permits.

PHILOCTETES: So soon, my son?

NEOPTOLEMUS:
 Why, yes. Watch for the weather on the spot,
 Not at a distance – that's the wisest way.

PHILOCTETES: Son, for your father's and your mother's sake,
 For the sake of all that's dear to you at home,
 Son, I beseech you, do not leave me here
 Alone and helpless in the sorry state
 In which you see me now – this wretched life
 That I have told you of! Do something, anything!
 I'm not an easy cargo – well I know it.
 But try to bear with me; a noble nature
 Must hate mean action and delight in good.
 Think of the shame if you refuse! O son,

Think of the honour that will crown your action
If I am brought alive to Oeta. O, do it!
Take me and stow me anywhere you will,
The hold, the bows, the steerage, anywhere
Where I shall give least trouble to the crew.
Say yes! I kneel before you, poor lame wretch
And crippled as I am ...

       (NEOPTOLEMUS *draws away from him.*)

No! Do not leave me
Alone again, so far from the track of man.
Take me but to your home, or to Euboea,
The home of Chalcodon; I will make my way,
Not far, to Oeta and the hills of Trachis,
Ay, to Spercheus, lovely river, there to see
My father – ah, but I fear, and long have feared
That I have lost him. Many and many a time
I sent him messages by those who passed,
Urgently praying him to send an escort
And fetch me home. But either he is dead,
Or else my messengers, as well may be,
Made light of my affair, and hurried home.
Now you can be my escort and my messenger.
Save me, for pity's sake! You must have pity
If you but think how all our mortal lives
Are set in danger and perplexity:
One day to prosper, and the next – who knows?
When all is well, then look for rocks ahead;
Look well to your life, when life runs easily;
Death may be waiting for you.

CHORUS: You cannot leave him, master,
  It's a pitiful tale he's told us
  Of pain past man's endurance.
  God keep the like from any friend of mine!
  For your grudge against your enemies,

I'd make that score a reason
For helping him, to spite them.
I'd take him aboard, sir, if I were you,
And ship him quick to the home he longs for,
Not tempt the anger of heaven.

NEOPTOLEMUS: It's all very well to be sympathetic now.
What if you change your mind on closer acquaintance,
Finding this pestilence more than you can bear?

CHORUS: No, sir, I'll never do that, I promise you.

NEOPTOLEMUS:
Well then, it shan't be said that I was less ready
Than you to help a friend in need. Come on, then.
We sail. He'd better follow as quick as he can.
The ship will hold him right enough. Pray God
We get off safe from here, then home at last.

PHILOCTETES: O joyful day! Kind sailors! Dearest friend!
If I could prove my gratitude in deeds –
But come, let's kiss goodbye to my old home:
Was ever such a home? See for yourself
The way I lived, and what I have endured.
The sight of it alone had been enough
For any lesser man. Only sheer need
Has taught me patience.

                He draws NEOPTOLEMUS *towards the cave.*

CHORUS: But stay, sir! What is this?
Two men approaching; one of ours, I think;
The other a stranger. Stay and hear their news
Before you go in yonder.

        Enter a MERCHANT SEAMAN, *whom we know to be*
        ODYSSEUS'S *man in disguise, with another sailor.*

MERCHANT: Son of Achilles? (NEOPTOLEMUS *stops and
moves towards him, leaving* PHILOCTETES *at a distance*).
My friend here that's come along with me – one of three
watchers by your ship – was good enough to tell me where

you'd be. 'Tis only by chance I've fallen in with you, when least expecting it, through happening to put in at this same coast. I'm homeward bound from Troy, sailing as master of a small freighter to Peparethus, the vineyard island; and when I heard that all these fellows were of your crew, I thought I couldn't go on my way without telling you some news I have, which you may think worth while to thank me for. Maybe you don't know the latest turn in your affairs; the Greeks have got new schemes against you; ay, more than schemes – deeds a-doing and moving fast.

NEOPTOLEMUS: I hope I shall not be ungrateful for your kindness, my friend. Tell me more. What are these Grecian schemes?

MERCHANT: Pursuers are already at sea and on your track, old Phoenix and the sons of Theseus.

NEOPTOLEMUS: Meaning to force me or to entice me back?

MERCHANT: I couldn't say. I only tell you what I have heard.

NEOPTOLEMUS: I suppose it is on behalf of the sons of Atreus that Phoenix and his crew are giving chase?

MERCHANT: Whether or no, it's being done, and quickly.

NEOPTOLEMUS: Strange that Odysseus was not ready to sail on the errand himself. What kept him back? Fear, eh?

MERCHANT: No; he and the son of Tydeus are gone in pursuit of someone else. They were setting out as I weighed anchor.

NEOPTOLEMUS: Whom were they after?

MERCHANT: A certain person – (*pretending to spy* PHILOC-TETES *for the first time*). But who's that yonder?

NEOPTOLEMUS: That –

MERCHANT: Speak low, sir.

NEOPTOLEMUS (*still for* PHILOCTETES *to hear*): That is none other than the famous Philoctetes.

MERCHANT (*feigning alarm*): Say no more, sir! Quick! Out of this country as soon as you can!

PHILOCTETES (*having by now dragged himself closer*): What is it, son? What bargain is he making there with you behind my back?

NEOPTOLEMUS: I don't know yet. Whatever it is, he'll have to make it openly to both of us.

MERCHANT (*pretending to cringe*): You'll not betray me to our people for saying more than I ought? I'm a poor man, and much beholden to them for fair treatment for my services.

NEOPTOLEMUS: But I am sworn enemy to the Atreidae, and this man is my dearest friend, because he hates them too. If you're here to do me good, you must tell us all you know and keep back nothing. Come, out with it.

MERCHANT: I warn you, young man.

NEOPTOLEMUS: I'm used to being on my guard.

MERCHANT: You'll only have yourself to blame.

NEOPTOLEMUS: Be it so. But speak.

MERCHANT: I will. These two I spoke of – the son of Tydeus
And great Odysseus – *this* is the man they're after,
Sworn by an oath to bring him, no matter how,
By force or by persuasion. Odysseus swore it
For all the Achaeans to hear, as bold as brass,
Cocksure he could do it – more so than the other.

NEOPTOLEMUS: What made the Atreidae, after all this time,
Think of this man whom they had cast away
So many years ago? What could they want?
Or was it the avenging power of the gods
Who punish wickedness?

MERCHANT: I can answer that.
Perhaps you never heard of a certain man
Born of the royal house, and skilled in prophecy,
Helenus, son of Priam? Well, one dark night,
Out goes the sly Odysseus by himself
(Was ever anything but evil said of him?),

Captures this Helenus by some trick or other,
And makes a public show of him to the Achaeans.
He, after prophesying this and that,
Tells them they'll never sack the towers of Troy
Until they've lured your friend by winning words
Back from this island where he makes his home.
Odysseus heard him and at once declared
He'd fetch the man, for all the Achaeans to see,
Thinking, most likely, he'd agree to come;
If not, he'd force him. 'This I'll do,' he said,
'Or any man of you can chop my head off.'
That's all, young man. If you take my advice,
You'll lose no time in getting on your way,
You and . . . anyone else you care about.

PHILOCTETES: O misery! That man, that prince of evil,
Swore he'd persuade me to go back with him,
Did he indeed? He might as soon persuade me
Back from the grave, the way his father came!

MERCHANT: Well, that's for you to say. I must be going
Back to my ship. Good luck be with you both.

Exit.

PHILOCTETES:
To think of the son of Laertes hoping to charm me
With subtle words, and bring me off his ship
In triumph before the eyes of all the Achaeans!
I'd sooner listen to my deadliest enemy
The viper, that did this mischief to my foot.
But he'd say anything, and dare to do it.
I know he'll soon be here. Come on, my son.
Oceans must separate us from Odysseus' ship;
And speed in season brings sound sleep at the end,
When the journey's over. Let us be going, my son.

NEOPTOLEMUS: All in good time. We cannot put to sea
Until this headwind drops. It's dead in our teeth.

PHILOCTETES:
All winds are fair, when death is on your heels.

NEOPTOLEMUS:
What keeps us back, keeps back the enemy too.

PHILOCTETES: No adverse wind keeps back the buccaneer
Bent upon robbery and plunder.

NEOPTOLEMUS: Well,
We'll go, then, as soon as you've got whatever you need
Or want to bring from yonder.

PHILOCTETES: There isn't much!
But some few things I need.

NEOPTOLEMUS: Is there anything
We can't supply on board?

PHILOCTETES: A certain herb
I have, which I mostly use to soothe this wound.
It gives me much relief.

NEOPTOLEMUS: Yes, bring it. What else?

PHILOCTETES: I may have left some arrows lying about.
I wouldn't like anyone else to pick *them* up.

NEOPTOLEMUS:
Is that the famous bow you have in your hand?

PHILOCTETES: It is – none other – this very one I hold.

NEOPTOLEMUS: May I look at it closer, handle it myself?
Salute it, rather, as a holy thing.

PHILOCTETES:
Of course; I would do anything for your satisfaction.

NEOPTOLEMUS: I'd dearly like to touch it; but – are you sure?
Is it permitted? If not, then . . . let it be.

PHILOCTETES:
You speak with reverence, my son. It is permitted.
You are my saviour; you have given me life,
Given me the hope of seeing my home again,
My friends, my father; you have raised me up
Above the enemies who trod me down.

Yes, you shall take the bow into your hands:
Touch it. Hold it. Now give it back to me.

(This little ceremony is solemnly performed,
NEOPTOLEMUS *almost hypnotized into obeying*
PHILOCTETES' *instructions.)*

And live to remember you are the only man
Thought worthy, for your goodness, so to do.
It was for goodness I myself was given it.
NEOPTOLEMUS: How glad I am to have found you, and
made you my friend!
To render kindness in return for kindness received
Is friendship above all price. Shall we go in?
PHILOCTETES: Yes, come. My sickness needs your care.
They go into the cave.

CHORUS:

The story was told
Of the fate that fell,
In an ancient time,
On a ravisher bold;
Whom the Father of All
For his impious crime
Bound fast on a wheel
In the fires of hell.

No other again
Has yet come near
To such misery,
Such endless pain;
Never has been
Such an agony
As the man we have seen
Has suffered here.

This fate he endured,
This wickedness,
Who had done no wrong
By force or fraud
To any on earth
His whole life long,
A lover of truth
And gentleness.

'Tis a wonder to know
How patiently
Year after year,
As the days of woe
Dragged slowly on,
He has lingered here,
Listening alone
To the sound of the sea.

Year after year,
In his empty lair,
Lamed and alone;
Not a creature near
To heed his cry;
Not a friend, not one
In the agony
His flesh must bear.

When the venomous brand
Burned hot in the veins
Of his ulcered limb,
No friend was at hand
To relieve that torture
And comfort him
With simples of nature
Soothing his pains.

To and fro
  On the barren ground,
Like a child without nurse
  He would slowly go
When the fit of his fever
  Had run its course,
Seeking whatever
  Might there be found.

No fruit of the earth
  For him might grow,
Such as human toil
  Brings yearly to birth
For our livelihood
  From the gentle soil;
His only food
  What fell to his bow.

Never a taste,
  These ten years long,
Of gladdening wine
  To quench his thirst;
Seeking some pool
  Of stagnant brine
For a draught to cool
  His parching tongue.

But the time is accomplished, a hero of noble birth is his
    friend,
Who shall carry him over the sea, to be happy and safe at
    the end,
In the house of the Malian maidens, Spercheus, and Oeta's
    height,
Where the Lord of the Bronze Shield reigns in the splendour
    of heavenly light.

Presently NEOPTOLEMUS *and* PHILOCTETES *return from the cave.* PHILOCTETES *is seized with a spasm of pain, and stops.* NEOPTOLEMUS, *ahead of him, does not at first notice this, but after a moment he turns.*

NEOPTOLEMUS:
  Come on, then. Why do you stand there dumb?

PHILOCTETES: Ah!

NEOPTOLEMUS: What is it?

PHILOCTETES: Nothing; go on, my boy.

NEOPTOLEMUS: Is the old wound troubling you again?

PHILOCTETES: No, nothing. It's better now ... O gods!

NEOPTOLEMUS: Why do you call so loud on the gods?

PHILOCTETES: I pray for their help and guidance ... Oh!

NEOPTOLEMUS: What is it? Tell me ... you must be in pain.

PHILOCTETES (*collapsing to the ground*):
  I'm done for ... no use trying to hide it.
  Oh! Oh! ... it goes right through me like a knife.
  I'm done for, boy ... it's come for me now ... (*racked with agony*) Pfff!
  Your sword, if you have it ... For God's sake, boy.
  Cut off my foot! Off with it! Quick!
  O son, O son! O let me die!

NEOPTOLEMUS: What is it? So suddenly coming upon
  you ... These terrible cries ...

PHILOCTETES: You know!

NEOPTOLEMUS: What is it?

PHILOCTETES: You know ...

NEOPTOLEMUS: Tell me, what is it?

PHILOCTETES: You must ... Ah!

NEOPTOLEMUS: It tortures you ...

PHILOCTETES: Torture ... I cannot tell you ... O for pity!

NEOPTOLEMUS: What can I do?

PHILOCTETES (*recovering a little*): Don't leave me now.
  There's nothing to fear.

The demon comes from time to time
After letting me alone for a little while.

NEOPTOLEMUS: I'm sorry to see you in such distress.
There seems no end to your troubles. Come,
Shall I give you a hand, or help you somehow?

PHILOCTETES: No. Take my bow, as you asked to do
Just now. Take it, and keep it for me
Until this bout of my pain is over.
As it passes, I shall fall into a sleep . . .
It is only then that the fever leaves me . . .
You must let me sleep it out. Remember,
If they come meanwhile, on your oath I bid you
Not give them the bow, on any account,
Nor ever let anyone take it from you.
If you do, it will mean your death and mine.
I am in your power: remember, I beseech you.

NEOPTOLEMUS: I'll take good care of it, never fear.
No one but you or I shall touch it.
Give it to me, and your blessing with it.

PHILOCTETES: Take it, my son. And pray that the gods,
In their jealousy, bring no such evil
On you, as they have dealt to me
And dealt to him that had it before me.

NEOPTOLEMUS:
May the gods hear both our prayers; and grant us
Sure sailing and swift to what place soever
Their favour and our set purpose guides us.

PHILOCTETES: My son, I fear that prayer will not be answered.
The dark blood oozes still from the deep vein.
I think there is more pain to come.
Oh! Oh! . . .
Curse you, foot; must you torment me so!
There it is again . . . now! . . . O the agony! . . .
You see how it is. No, do not run away.

O would to God this torment might be yours,
Odysseus of Cephallenia, piercing you
Through to the very heart! O there again!
If you could have been in my place, generals both,
Agamemnon and Menelaus, all this time!
O death, death, death, why can you never come?
Daily I call for you. O take me, son,
Kind son, take me and throw me into the flames
Of the fire that lights up Lemnos. It was there
I steeled myself to do the same to Heracles,
The son of Zeus; those weapons which you hold
I won for the service. What do you say, my son?
Nothing? Are you there? Do you say nothing, son?

NEOPTOLEMUS: I am too much troubled at your suffering.

PHILOCTETES:
Let it not trouble you. It comes upon me suddenly,
Then goes as quickly. Only, I beseech you,
Don't leave me alone.

NEOPTOLEMUS: I won't, I promise you.

PHILOCTETES: You'll stay?

NEOPTOLEMUS: Of course.

PHILOCTETES: You swear? I must not ask it.

NEOPTOLEMUS: It is impossible I should go without you.

PHILOCTETES: Your hand on it.

NEOPTOLEMUS: My hand. I stay with you.

PHILOCTETES (rolling his eyes feebly towards the cave):
Up there! Up there!

NEOPTOLEMUS: Where? What do you mean?

PHILOCTETES: Up there!

NEOPTOLEMUS: Why do you gaze upon the sky above us?

PHILOCTETES: I must go there . . . let me go.

NEOPTOLEMUS (restraining him): Where?

PHILOCTETES: Let me go.

NEOPTOLEMUS: No, no.

PHILOCTETES: Do you want to kill me? Let me go.

NEOPTOLEMUS (*releasing him*):

Go, then, if you can manage by yourself.

PHILOCTETES (*falling to the ground again*):

O Earth, receive me, I must die this instant.

I can stand no longer ... O the pain, the pain!

NEOPTOLEMUS: I think he will soon sleep. His head droops.

He sweats from head to foot, and the blood wells in a dark
stream from his heel. Let us leave him in peace, men; leave
him to sleep.

CHORUS: Come down, sweet sleep,

Wherein there is no memory of pain,

No suffering.

Come, happy, happy sleep

All-conquering.

Hold thou before his eyes

The light of peace that now begins to fill them.

Come, sleep, we pray, O come

With healing wing.

(PHILOCTETES *sleeps*.)

Now, sir, what will you do?

What shall our plan be now ?

Look, sir, he sleeps; why do we wait?

Luck's the master of all; take it and win.

NEOPTOLEMUS:

He does not hear us, certain; and we have got his bow;

But that's no use to us, if we sail off without him.

The victory must be his; the god said we must bring him.

How shall we look, our task half done, and that by fraud?

CHORUS: Leave that to heaven.

But softly, softly; better not speak so loud

Lest he should stir.

For often after pain

The sufferer

Will sleep but fitfully;
And who knows what he may not hear or see
In his uneasiness?
  Speak softly, sir.
Do what you have to do
While he's asleep, say I.
You know my meaning. The other way,
It's plain to see, brings mischief on us all.
The wind is ours, the man lies here asleep,
Ay, sound asleep in the sun, blind and helpless,
As good as dead. He can't move hand or foot,
Defenceless.
What are you thinking of?
Go while the going's good,
Is my advice.

NEOPTOLEMUS:
  Be silent, fool! His eyes are opening. He moves.

PHILOCTETES: The light . . . I am awake again . . .
And O, more than I hoped . . . my faithful friends
Still watching over me. I had not dared,
My son, to think that you would still be here
Patiently waiting on my sufferings,
Ready to help and pity me. This was more
Than our good lords, the Atreidae, ever did.
They could not bear it. You are a true nobleman
To endure it all so bravely, the cries, the foulness,
Which I have afflicted you with.
Come then, my son;
Now that I am allowed a little breathing-space
To forget the demon, lift me – you, my son –
And set me on my feet. As soon as may be,
If the weakness leaves me, we'll away to ship,
And then to sea.

NEOPTOLEMUS: O my good friend, I'm glad.

I never thought to see you alive again
And free from pain. To all appearances,
With all you had suffered, you were marked for death.
Stand up. Or shall these fellows carry you?
If you and I desire it, they'll be ready.

PHILOCTETES:
Thanks, son. Yes, lift me up – but you, not they –
They need not bear with my condition yet;
Living on board with me will be their trial.

NEOPTOLEMUS:
Just as you will. Stand up. Give me your hand.

PHILOCTETES:
You'll see. I'll stand as well as ever ... There!

NEOPTOLEMUS: But now ... O now, what shall I do?

PHILOCTETES: Why, son?
What do you mean?

NEOPTOLEMUS: How can I tell you, how?

PHILOCTETES:
How tell me what? My son, you cannot mean –

NEOPTOLEMUS:
But something must be told. Now is the time.

PHILOCTETES: Is it my wounds – the intolerable offence
Has proved too much for you – you cannot take me?

NEOPTOLEMUS:
The offence is here! A man betraying himself
To do such deeds as are not of his nature!

PHILOCTETES: You? But all you have done, all you have said
To help your honest friend, is true to yourself
And to your noble father.

NEOPTOLEMUS: I shall be known
For the wretched thing I am: this was my torment.

PHILOCTETES: Not in this action. But I fear your meaning.

NEOPTOLEMUS: O God, what shall I do? Deceitful twice,
Twice false, whether I speak or hold my tongue.

PHILOCTETES: I do believe the man will go and leave me!
NEOPTOLEMUS:
  No! Leave you, never! No, this is my torment,
  That I must take you, it may be to your death.
PHILOCTETES: My son, I do not understand.
NEOPTOLEMUS: Then plainly:
  It is to Troy that you must sail, to the Achaeans,
  To the army which the Atreidae lead.
PHILOCTETES: No, no!
NEOPTOLEMUS: But listen –
PHILOCTETES: Why? What will you do with me?
NEOPTOLEMUS:
  First, save you from this wretchedness; and then –
  Then we must make Troy tremble, you and I.
PHILOCTETES: You mean to do this?
NEOPTOLEMUS: Forgive me; I have no choice.

PHILOCTETES: O, I am lost, betrayed! By you, sir! Why?
  Come, give me back my bow.
NEOPTOLEMUS: I cannot do that. I must obey my masters
  For duty's sake and for my own.
PHILOCTETES: O fiend!
  Monster, quintessence of vilest duplicity!
  Have you done this to me? Played me this trick?
  And can you face me unashamed, your suppliant
  Who crawled to you for pity? Heart of stone!
  You take my bow from me, you take my life.
  O give it back to me, son, give it back to me!
  (Gods of our fathers!) Give me back my life! ...
  He will not hear ... not speak ... he turns away.
  He will not give it back ...
    Then I must speak to you, seas, rocks and headlands,
  And all my creatures of the hills; to you,
  My old companions, I must cry again;
  Who else will hear?

Hear what Achilles' son will do to me!
He swore his oath that he would take me home;
To Troy he takes me. Swore with his hand in mine;
And now that hand has robbed me of my bow,
The immortal bow I had from Heracles
The son of Zeus; and he will flourish it
Boasting among the Argives.
As if I had the power to struggle against him,
He drags me forcibly away. Does he not see
He fights a ghost, a shadow that has no substance?
If only I had my strength! Even as I am,
It needed treachery to take me. Tricked,
And beaten! Tell me, tell me what to do! ...
                    (*Again to* NEOPTOLEMUS)
O be yourself again. Give it me back ...
No answer? ... Silent? ... This, then, is the end.

Back to my cranny in the rocks, up there,
Back I must go, disarmed, to wither up
And die alone there, if I have no bow
To kill a bird or beast with. I shall be
The prey now, carrion food for those I fed on.
The hunted will come hunting for my carcase,
Demanding blood for blood, the price of murder.
This is my reward for trusting one who seemed
Incapable of guile.

                    (*To* NEOPTOLEMUS)
Die! Die!
Unless I may yet see you change your purpose?
No? Then die a coward's death!
CHORUS: What now, sir?
    'Tis you to give the word: are we to sail,
    Or listen to his prayers?
NEOPTOLEMUS: Strange, how I pity him,

As I have always done.

PHILOCTETES: Have mercy, son!
By all the gods, have mercy; or the world
Will hate you for the trick you play on me.

NEOPTOLEMUS: What shall I do? Why did I ever leave
Scyros, to come to this predicament?

PHILOCTETES: I know there is no wickedness in you.
The part you have come here to play was taught you,
I think, by wicked men. Leave it to them.
Give me my weapon, and go.

NEOPTOLEMUS: What think you, friends?

> ODYSSEUS, *who has come upon the scene in time to*
> *see* NEOPTOLEMUS *on the point of yielding, now*
> *intervenes with a shout.*

ODYSSEUS: Traitor! What are you at? Give *me* the bow.
Stand back!

PHILOCTETES: Great heaven! Odysseus do I hear?

ODYSSEUS: You do, and see him.

PHILOCTETES: Sold to my death! O God!
I knew it, *he* worked this scheme to rob me.

ODYSSEUS: Yes! I did it; who else?

PHILOCTETES (*to* NEOPTOLEMUS): The bow, lad! Give
me the bow.

ODYSSEUS: Never. And you must go where *it* goes. March!
Or must we force you?

PHILOCTETES: Force me, insolent!

ODYSSEUS: Come willingly, then.

PHILOCTETES: O Lemnos, and almighty king Volcano,
Do you see this? Must I be dragged away
A prisoner before your eyes?

ODYSSEUS: The will of Zeus.
He is this country's king, and I am his officer.

PHILOCTETES:
You lie, foul villain, making God's word a lie

To shield your practices.

ODYSSEUS: No lie, sir. March!

PHILOCTETES: Never.

ODYSSEUS: You shall. And I must be obeyed.

PHILOCTETES: There is no help then. To this end was I born, a slave for all my days.

ODYSSEUS: That is not so. You are, and shall be, the equal of the bravest, with whom you are to conquer Troy and bring it to destruction.

PHILOCTETES: No, I say; let me suffer what I may; this island's highest pinnacle shall serve me yet.

ODYSSEUS: What now?

PHILOCTETES: What if I leap from a rocky height to dash myself to pieces on the rocks below?

ODYSSEUS: Hold him! Prevent him!

PHILOCTETES (*overpowered after a brief struggle*): Ah, helpless hands; a prisoner. O my beloved bow, where are you? . . . So, sir, once again you have stolen a march on me; when was there anything but deceit and depravity in your soul? Once again you have trapped me, making this boy your stalking-horse. I did not know him till today, but now I know he is one of my sort, not of yours. He had no thought but to carry out his orders; and already it is plain he is sorry for his error and for the wrong done to me. It was your vile mind that lurked behind the loophole and schooled his unwilling innocence to this proficiency in guile. Once you flung me, a helpless homeless outcast on this shore, flung me into a living death; and now you mean to drag me back, a prisoner. May the gods destroy you! How often have I prayed it. But the gods have no good gifts for me; and there you stand, rejoicing in life, while every breath of life I draw is agony and torment, my sufferings your sport – you and the Atreid pair, your masters in this business. And how came you to be harnessed to their

team? Only by force and a cunning trick; while I, fool that
I was, came of my own free will, with my seven ships, only
to be abused and thrown aside; their work, say you – they
call it yours. And now, what do you want of me? Why do
you seize me and carry me away? I am nothing, long dead
to you. God's plagues upon you, am I not still the poisonous
infected wretch I was? What of your sacrifices to the
blessed gods, if I am of your crew? What of the pollution
of your drink-offerings? Such was the pretext on which
you banished me; does it not still hold good? Go to your
miserable death, as surely you will, for what you did to me,
if there is any justice in heaven. Ay, and I know there is.
Only the whip in the hand of God could have driven you on
this quest for one so wretched as I. O my country, and you
unsleeping gods, if you have any pity still, bring vengeance,
vengeance, late though it be, on all my persecutors!
Misery is my life, yet if I might but live to see them perish,
I could believe my torture ended.

CHORUS: Stubborn as ever, sir; and these stubborn words
Show that he's in no mind to accept defeat.

ODYSSEUS: I could answer him; but this is not the time.

(*To* PHILOCTETES)

This will I say: I am as I need to be;
Where honour and truth are at stake, I can show myself
The equal of any. Whatever the contest be,
I must have victory – except in this one;
Here I give way to you.
– Release him, then.
Let no one touch him; leave him where he is –
We have your weapon, that is all we want.
Teucer is with us, and he will know how to use it;
Or my own hand and eye may prove to be
No worse than yours. We need not trouble you.
You're welcome to the length and breadth of Lemnos;

And we must go. Since you refuse the honour
Your treasure should have brought you, let it be mine.
PHILOCTETES: What shall I do? Am I to think of you
   Parading my weapons among the Greeks?
ODYSSEUS: Enough. I am going.
PHILOCTETES (*to* NEOPTOLEMUS):
   Son of Achilles, will you go too
   Without a word?
ODYSSEUS: Not a look, or we lose our fortune;
   I know your noble nature.
PHILOCTETES (*to the sailors*): And you, my friends?
   Have I lost your pity? Will you desert me too?
CHORUS: This lad is our master, sir, his word is ours.
NEOPTOLEMUS:
   Stay here, men. I shall be called too tender-hearted
   By my commander; but stay, if he will allow you,
   Till the crew have got our gear in order for sailing
   And we have made our prayers. Maybe our friend
   By that time will have come to think better of us.
   We two will go, and you be ready to follow
   As soon as we send you word; come quickly then.
            Exeunt ODYSSEUS *and* NEOPTOLEMUS.

PHILOCTETES: My stony house, my cave,
   Sun-hot, ice-cold, to be
   My dwelling-place for ever,
   And now my grave.
   Home of my misery,
   How shall I live, where turn
   For my provisioning?
   The birds above my head
   Are free as the winds that sing,
   And my strength fled.
CHORUS: It was your doing, unhappy man;

No other forced you to it, none.
You could have chosen a wiser way;
You chose the worse.

PHILOCTETES: This is the fate that I
Must live with here, alone
In pain and wretchedness
Until I die,
My arrows fly no more,
My hand is powerless
To find my daily bread.
Tricked by a hidden lie!
O that my enemy, day for day,
Might bear my agony!

CHORUS; The act of heaven, no treachery
Of ours, has brought you to this end.
Curse others if you will; my wish
Is still to be your friend.

PHILOCTETES: And he
Sits laughing by the sea,
My weapon in his hands,
My darling bow
Which no man ever touched
But I. Beloved bow,
Torn from these hands that loved you,
Do you not know,
Not feel with sadness
That the friend of Heracles
Shall never handle you again?
Now a new master, master of deceit,
Is yours to serve.
And O, what treachery,
What wickedness
You must now see –
That hated man,

Whose shamelessness
A thousand times, O God,
Has here tormented me!

CHORUS: A man should speak up for the right,
I'd say, but not unleash his tongue
To spiteful insults. He you revile
Came at the bidding of his people
To do a service for his friends.

PHILOCTETES: You birds that fly,
Whom once I made my sport,
And beasts that stare
Bright-eyed upon the hills,
No longer do I hunt you down,
No longer bear
The arrows in which I trusted.
This is my end,
And you are free;
Here is no more to fear;
Here is your just revenge,
Blood for the blood I shed,
My rotting flesh
For you to feed on.
How shall I live? Will air
Support me, having no power
To win life from the lap of mother earth?

CHORUS: Man, by whatever gods you fear,
You cannot turn from such a friend
Who comes to treat you kindly. Think,
Freedom is in your hands,
Escape from the devil that drives you, devours you
With endless torture beyond endurance.

PHILOCTETES:
Must you, my kindest friend, torture me again and again
With the old scourge? Why must you treat me so?

CHORUS: We? How?

PHILOCTETES: You talk of the hated land of Troy
And mean to take me there.

CHORUS: We think it best.

PHILOCTETES: Away, away!

CHORUS: So be it. We're ready enough.
There's work for us.
Come, lads, away.

PHILOCTETES: Stay!
O, as you fear God's wrath –

CHORUS: Gently, sir.

PHILOCTETES: Stay; for God's sake, stay.

CHORUS: What now?

PHILOCTETES: O, I am in hell.
What shall I do, accursed foot,
What shall I do with you
From now until I die? . . .
Come back, my friends, come back!

CHORUS: Have you changed your mind?
You told us to go. What now?

PHILOCTETES: I don't know what I am saying.
Pain drowns my senses.
Do not be angry, friends.

CHORUS: Come now, do as we say, poor man.

PHILOCTETES: No, no! That's certain; I will not go,
Though thunder and lightning burn me up.
Cursed be Troy and the men that fight there,
The men that could fling me helpless here! . . .
Do one thing for me.

CHORUS: What?

PHILOCTETES: A sword,
An axe, a weapon of any sort,
If you have one, quickly –

CHORUS: What to do? Some violence, I'll be bound.

PHILOCTETES: Yes! Hack myself to pieces, limb from limb!
   What should I want but death –

CHORUS: Why?

PHILOCTETES: And to find my father –

CHORUS: Where?

PHILOCTETES: In the land of the dead, for there he surely is.
   O home and country! Never to see you again!
   Fool, to have left that holy river; fool,
   To join myself to the Greeks, my hated enemies!
   Now let me die . . .
           He crawls away to his cave.

CHORUS:
   We should have been off and away to the ship by now:
   But look, here comes Odysseus, and the Captain.
     Enter ODYSSEUS *and* NEOPTOLEMUS.

ODYSSEUS: Why have you hurried back again like this?

NEOPTOLEMUS: To undo the wrong that I have already done.

ODYSSEUS:
   I don't understand. What wrong are you talking about?

NEOPTOLEMUS:
   In obeying your orders and those of all the army –

ODYSSEUS:
   In obeying them you did nothing you need be ashamed of.

NEOPTOLEMUS:
   I used base treachery against a fellow-creature.

ODYSSEUS:
   What! Heavens! You mean you've got some crazy scheme –

NEOPTOLEMUS:
   No crazy scheme; but a debt to the son of Poeas.

ODYSSEUS: My God! Can I believe my ears? You mean –

NEOPTOLEMUS:
   To restore this bow to the man I took it from.

ODYSSEUS: You're mad. You cannot be going to give it back.

NEOPTOLEMUS:

I am, for I got it unfairly, and have no right to it.

ODYSSEUS: Are you joking?

NEOPTOLEMUS: One doesn't speak the truth for a joke.

ODYSSEUS:

Neoptolemus, what do you mean? Tell me what you mean.

NEOPTOLEMUS:

I've told you. How many more times must I repeat it?

ODYSSEUS: Once is enough: too much.

NEOPTOLEMUS: Then that is all.

ODYSSEUS:

There is a power that can stop you doing this crazy thing.

NEOPTOLEMUS: What power? Who'll stop me?

ODYSSEUS: The whole Achaean army,

And I among them.

NEOPTOLEMUS: The wise Odysseus is talking like a fool.

ODYSSEUS: You're not only talking but acting like a fool.

NEOPTOLEMUS: Justice is sometimes better than wisdom.

ODYSSEUS: Justice!

To throw away what I have helped you to win?

NEOPTOLEMUS:

I have acted unjustly and mean to make amends.

ODYSSEUS:

And don't you fear the wrath of the Achaean army?

NEOPTOLEMUS:

With justice on my side, I don't fear anything

That you can do.

ODYSSEUS: Indeed!

NEOPTOLEMUS: Do what you will.

ODYSSEUS: So I must fight with you, instead of with Trojans?

NEOPTOLEMUS: I am ready.

ODYSSEUS: With the sword, then. Here is mine (*drawing*).

NEOPTOLEMUS: And mine (*drawing*).

A pause: ODYSSEUS *sheathes his sword.*

ODYSSEUS: I'll not waste time with you. I'm going back.
Our men shall hear of this; yes, every man,
And they'll know how to deal with you.

NEOPTOLEMUS: Much wiser.
Be so in future, and keep clear of trouble.
(*Exit* ODYSSEUS.)
Philoctetes! Philoctetes, are you there
In your sepulchre? Come out!

PHILOCTETES *appears at the mouth of the cave.*

PHILOCTETES: Who calls me now?
Who is it? What do you want? ... O, more iniquity!
Have you come to torment me again?

NEOPTOLEMUS: There's nothing to fear.
Listen –

PHILOCTETES: I listened to you once before,
And what but evil came of all your talking?

NEOPTOLEMUS: Is not repentance possible?

PHILOCTETES: You said as much
When you planned to steal my bow; your seeming honesty
Was all deception.

NEOPTOLEMUS: It is not so now.
Tell me, are you still determined to remain,
Or will you come with me?

PHILOCTETES: I'll hear no more!
You waste your breath.

NEOPTOLEMUS: You are determined?

PHILOCTETES: Yes;
More than determined.

NEOPTOLEMUS: I wish I could persuade you;
But if I cannot – (*he turns away*).

PHILOCTETES: No, nothing that you can say
Can turn me now. You take away my life,
Rob me by trickery, and back you come again
To give me advice. The son of such a father!

Go to your deaths, the pack of you, Atreus' sons,
Laertes' son, and you!

PHILOCTETES: Stop. Curse no more.

NEOPTOLEMUS: Stop. Curse no more.
Here is your bow . . .

PHILOCTETES: What? . . . Is this another trick?

NEOPTOLEMUS: No trick, I swear by God in his heaven.

PHILOCTETES: If true,
This is most wonderful.

NEOPTOLEMUS:
The deed will prove it true. Here is your bow.
Take it. It is yours.

> As PHILOCTETES *takes the bow,* ODYSSEUS *reappears*
> *at a distance.*

ODYSSEUS: By God, he shall not have it!
I speak for the Atreidae and all the Grecian army;
And I forbid it.

PHILOCTETES: Is that Odysseus' voice?

ODYSSEUS: It is. Let the son of Achilles say what he will,
This time I mean to take you back to Troy.

PHILOCTETES (*preparing to shoot*):
Not if this arrow finds its mark.

NEOPTOLEMUS (*arresting his hand*): No, no!
For God's sake!

PHILOCTETES: Let me go, I say!
For God's sake, boy!

NEOPTOLEMUS: I cannot.

> ODYSSEUS *escapes.*

PHILOCTETES: Ah, too late.
You let my bitterest enemy escape.
This arrow could have killed him.

NEOPTOLEMUS: To have done it
Would have been unworthy of yourself or me.

PHILOCTETES: Well, well. It's easy to see what cowards they
are,

These officers, self-styled ambassadors,
When it comes to a fight, for all their mighty talk.

NEOPTOLEMUS:
True. And the bow is yours. Am I forgiven?

PHILOCTETES: You are; and once more true to your parent-
    age,
Not like a son of Sisyphus, but of Achilles.
No name stood higher than his, of all men living,
Nor now of all the dead.

NEOPTOLEMUS:
I am grateful for your praise of my father, and of myself.
But now I must ask you to listen to a request.
Each one of us must live the life God gives him;
It cannot be shirked; but there is no excuse,
Nor pity, for those who choose to cling to suffering
And hardship of their own making, as you would do.
You have shut your heart, and will listen to no advice;
Those who attempt to persuade you, in all goodwill,
Are met with hostility, hatred, and suspicion.
Even so, I'll say what I have to say, God help me.
Mark it, and write it on your soul.
    This plague you suffer is a judgement sent from heaven,
For having trespassed on the domain of Chryse,
And encountered her sentinel, the secret watcher,
The serpent that guards her open sanctuary.
From this affliction there is no escape for you,
So long as the sun travels from east to west,
Until you come, of your own accord, to Troy.
There you will find the sons of Asclepius,
Who are with us, and there you will find relief from pain.
And then, with this bow, and in alliance with me,
Troy's fall must be your triumph, for all to see.
How do I know it? We have a Trojan prisoner,
Helenus, a notable prophet, who has pronounced

That this must come to pass; and furthermore,
That Troy is doomed to fall this very summer;
He has staked his life on it.
Now, knowing this,
Refuse no longer. Think what you have to gain;
You are chosen champion of the Greeks; skilled hands
Will heal your trouble, and then – the glorious honour
Of ending the dolorous tale of Troy with victory.

PHILOCTETES: O why am I condemned to live so long?
Can I not die? Ye gods, can I not die?
What can I do? I cannot turn deaf ears
To my kind counsellor. But can I go
From this long wretchedness back to the light of day,
Back to the sight of men? Can eyes of mine,
Seeing such things as they have seen, see this,
My meeting again those two, my murderers,
And the evil-hearted son of Laertes? ... No,
It is not the thought of what is past that sours me,
But what is yet to come. I can foresee it.
The soul that has conceived one wickedness
Can nurse no good thereafter.
What of yourself?
Your motive in this business
Is strange. You never should have gone to Troy,
Much less attempt to get me there. They mocked you,
You said, refusing you your father's arms,
And even put poor Ajax below Odysseus;
And now you want to go and fight for them,
And make me do the same? You cannot do it.
My son, you swore upon your solemn oath
To take me home. Do that. Then go to Scyros,
And leave these wretches to their wretched deaths.
For this I shall be twice indebted to you,
As will my father. Do you want to brand yourself

With the villainy to which you lend your aid?

NEOPTOLEMUS: Believe me, I understand. But yet I beg you
To trust in the gods, and in my promises,
And come with me, as with a friend.

PHILOCTETES: To Troy?
To meet a son of Atreus? And in this state,
Cursed with this foulness in my foot?

NEOPTOLEMUS: But no,
You will find there those who will heal the ulcered limb,
And set you free.

PHILOCTETES: Do you mean that, serpent's tongue?

NEOPTOLEMUS: I mean what I judge best for both of us.

PHILOCTETES: Shameless as ever?

NEOPTOLEMUS: Why should I be ashamed
To help my friends?

PHILOCTETES: What friends? The Atreidae? Or me?

NEOPTOLEMUS:
Why, you. Have I not told you I am your friend?

PHILOCTETES: And mean to give me over to my enemies?

NEOPTOLEMUS:
So obstinate still, in the face of all misfortune?

PHILOCTETES: I know you; you want to lure me to my death.

NEOPTOLEMUS: Not I; you do not understand.

PHILOCTETES: Who else,
If not the sons of Atreus, banished me?
Not understand, indeed!

NEOPTOLEMUS: I know they banished you:
But now, you'll see, they'll bring you back to life.

PHILOCTETES: Not if I know it. I'll not set eyes on Troy
For anything in the world.

NEOPTOLEMUS (*giving it up*): What is the use, then,
Of all my talking, if nothing I can say
Will change your mind? I'd better say no more,
And you must go on living, as you are,

This hopeless helpless life.

PHILOCTETES: As for my sufferings, let me bear them still,
So far as is appointed. But once again,
I ask you this, my son: you have given your promise,
Our hands on it, to see me safely home.
Will you do this, my son? You promised it.
Will you do it now, and never speak again
The name of Troy? For I have wept enough . . .

NEOPTOLEMUS *is torn for some moments by an inward struggle:
at last he speaks with a changed and resolute tone.*

NEOPTOLEMUS: Yes, let us go.

PHILOCTETES: O bravely spoken!

NEOPTOLEMUS: Step out, then, firmly.

PHILOCTETES: As well as I can.

NEOPTOLEMUS: The Achaeans will make it hot for me!

PHILOCTETES: You needn't fear.

NEOPTOLEMUS: They'll sack my country.

PHILOCTETES: I shall be there.

NEOPTOLEMUS: What can you do?

PHILOCTETES: The arrows of Heracles –

NEOPTOLEMUS: The bow!

PHILOCTETES: The bow will keep them at their distance.

*They are now on the point of disappearing from the
scene:* HERACLES *appears above.*

NEOPTOLEMUS: So, take your last farewell of Lemnos.

HERACLES: Stay! Son of Poeas, stay and hear!
It is the voice of Heracles,
It is his form you see.
I am come from my high seat
In heaven above.
This is the will of Zeus:
The journey which you now intend,
You must not go.
Hear me.

Hear first my history; glorious immortality
Is mine, won by great labours bravely borne;
And I am as you see me now. So you
Must win, it is ordained, through suffering
Glory in life. You are to go to Troy
With him; you are to have your sickness cured;
You are to be the chosen champion
Of that great army; you are to seek out Paris,
First cause of all this wickedness, and destroy him
With those, my weapons; you are to sack the city
And carry home the spoils, the award of honour,
To Oeta, to delight your father's eyes;
And there, upon my altar, dedicate
A portion, in remembrance of the bow.

　　Son of Achilles, here are words for you:
You cannot conquer Troy without his help,
Nor he without you. Guard each other's life,
Like lions hunting together. Asclepius,
Whom I shall send to Troy, will be your healer.
And then, for the second time, as is ordained,
My arrows bring the city down. Remember,
In the hour of victory, reverence to the gods.
This is the thing our Father holds most precious;
And piety does not perish when men die;
They live and die, but it must live for ever.

PHILOCTETES: The very voice
　That I have longed to hear!
　The face
　As once I knew it!
　I shall not disobey.

NEOPTOLEMUS: Nor I.

HERACLES: Then lose no time; the wind is fair
　For your adventure.
　　　　　　　　He disappears.

PHILOCTETES: So, farewell
  To Lemnos, and my cave, my watchtower.
  Farewell to Nymphs of riverside
  And field; and to the deep male music
  Of sea and rock, where winds have driven
  The spray in showers about my head
  Beneath my very roof, and yonder
  The Hill of Hermes heard my voice
  Echo above the storm. Farewell,
  Fresh brooks, and Lycian spring, farewell.
  At last I leave you. This is the day
  I never thought to see. Goodbye,
  Lemnos, my island; wish me well
  And speed this voyage which I must make
  Obedient to my fate, my friends,
  And the Great God who wills it so.

CHORUS:
  Come all; and let us pray
  The Nymphs that rule the sea
  This day
  To guard and guide us happily
  Upon our homeward way.

EXEUNT

P. 22   *Chorus:* this title is applied, throughout the plays, to lines which may be spoken either chorally or by a leader or other individual speakers.

P. 32   *Aias* is the Greek form of the name more familiar as Ajax, and is associated here with 'Aiai' as a cry of woe. What we should perhaps call a pun could have for the Greeks a more solemn or superstitious significance, implying that the name had some kind of necessary connexion with the fate of its owner. Something of the same kind occurs below with reference to the name of the child, Eurysaces (Broad-shield).

P. 41   *Cyllene:* a mountain in Arcadia, the birthplace of Hermes and of Pan, his son.

      Nysian: the name Nysa was given to various places in Greece, Asia Minor, Africa, and Arabia, and is connected with the name and cult of Dionysus. An alternative reading 'Mysian' is also found.

      Cnosian: of Cnosus (Knossos) in Crete.

P. 45   The death of Ajax is of course assumed to take place in a secluded spot at some distance from the camp. The Greek theatre may have had some means of indicating a change of scene; but the difficulty of dispensing with it is not as great as it used to appear to commentators whose imagination was limited to the convention of 'realistic' theatre. On the modern stage a short interval and slight change of setting would be possible but by no means essential.

P. 73 *Itys*: the song of the nightingale was commonly a symbol of grief, the bird Philomela being supposed to lament for her lost child Itys.

Iphianassa: Homer gives Agamemnon three daughters, Chrysothemis, Laodice (Electra), and Iphianassa, the last being generally identified with Iphigeneia who was sacrificed at Aulis. Sophocles, however, evidently assumes that there were four daughters.

P. 83 *Pelops' chariot-wheels*: Pelops, an ancestor of Agamemnon, competed in a chariot race against Oenomaus, king of Pisa, to win the hand of his daughter. By one account, Myrtilus the charioteer of Oenomaus tampered with his master's vehicle so as to give the victory to Pelops, but later, incurring the enmity of Pelops, was hurled by him into the sea. It would seem that Sophocles has some slightly different version of the story in mind.

P. 93 *There was a king*: the point of the instance is to show example for the dead being avenged on the living murderer. Amphiaraus, an Argive prince, was persuaded by his wife Eriphyle, whom Polyneices rewarded with a golden necklace, to join the expedition of the 'Seven' against Thebes (cf. *Oedipus at Colonus*). In the flight of the vanquished host from Thebes, Amphiaraus was swallowed alive in an earthquake. Sophocles wrote a tragedy and a satyric play on this subject.

P. 97 *To help me kill the man*: it is characteristic of this play that the problem of matricide is soft-pedalled. The death of Aegisthus is given prominence as the climax of the play, and we are almost led to suppose that Clytaemnestra might have escaped if she had happened to be out of the way at the critical moment. Yet, when the moment comes, Electra is vehement for her mother's death; and indeed it has been clear all along that her hatred of her is mitigated by no sense of filial duty or moral scruple. It is not difficult to agree with Sophocles' feeling that Electra would shrink from revealing to her sister the full horror of the deed on which her heart was set.

P. 100 *Will we not learn?* The Chorus are not, of course, supporting Chrysothemis. The 'debt to parents' in this case excludes the guilty parent: a rather grimly unfortunate piece of moralizing, in the circumstances.

P. 107   *O light, O joy:* from the recognition onwards, the swiftness
          and economy of the drama, and the justice of its psychology,
          show Sophocles at his most masterly. Orestes faces his task
          loyally, but with no vindictive pleasure – rather with an in-
          creasing distaste and a hint of misgiving. Electra, almost un-
          hinged by the sudden revelation of good fortune, looses all the
          pent-up flood of her passion to sweep him on to the hateful
          act.

P. 114   *If Apollo was right:* if Sophocles meant to carry our thoughts
          forward to a further chapter in the history of Orestes, and the
          coming torments of his guilt-ridden conscience, he has done it
          with the barest possible hint. The closing lines of the play sug-
          gest nothing but finality. To those who complain that the
          author has shirked the vital issue, the best answer on his behalf
          seems to be that he was not, like Aeschylus, writing a trilogy,
          and his artistic sense preferred a compact and completed story
          to any suggestion of a sequel. What happened afterwards could
          if necessary be made the subject of a new play. And the
          Chorus, in any case, are not infallible judges.

P. 119   *Trachis*, the scene of the play, is a town on the Malian Gulf, between Thermopylae and the mouth of the river Spercheus. Some twenty miles out to sea, beyond the narrow entrance to the gulf, lies the north-westerly tip of the long island of Euboea, the point at which Heracles is reported to have paused on his homeward journey. The time allowed for the passage of the various persons to and fro between these two places, and for the intervening incidents, would seem to strain dramatic licence to an excessive degree if we considered the play as a continuous action; it is rather to be read as a sequence of episodes separated by indefinite lapses of time.

Deianeira is a native of western Greece, the region where the river Achelous forms a boundary between Aetolia and Acarnania. On her marriage with Heracles, she had lived at Tiryns, near Argos, until after his encounter with Iphitus, when they became 'exiles' under the protection of Ceyx, king of Trachis.

Other geographical features alluded to in the play are Mount Oeta, standing above the valley of the Spercheus, and the Hot Springs near Thermopylae.

P. 123   *Scion of Cadmus:* Heracles had been born at Thebes and virtually adopted into the royal house of that city.

P. 124   *Dove-priestesses:* there are various interpretations of this term (*Peleiades*) – doves – grey-haired ones – speakers with dovelike voices – interpreters of omens given by doves. Here and in the words of Heracles (p. 158) Sophocles refers to the legend that an oracle was given either by the agency of the doves or by the rustling of the leaves of the sacred oak. Dodona, in N.W. Greece, was from the earliest times and through many centuries a site dedicated to Zeus. Herodotus (II.54) has an explicit account of the dove-legend connected with this shrine.

P. 134   *By the fires of God:* the construction put upon this speech is of some importance in relation to the character of Deianeira. It has been asked whether she is sincere in this profession of forgiveness, or is only using diplomacy to get the truth from Lichas. I cannot think – if Sophocles' pen has been true to his intention – that the opening words of the speech are consistent with a studied insincerity. Further, though a passing mood of exasperation betrays itself in a later speech, the whole aim of Deianeira's plan is to recover her husband's love, not to visit him with any retribution. Her forgiveness of Iole naturally partakes more of pity than of love.

P. 137   *They fought*: the text here is corrupt and the abrupt conclusion of the ode perhaps preserves only fragments of the author's original intention.

P. 138   *Lernaean Hydra*: Heracles had encountered and destroyed the Hydra, a serpentine monster, in the marsh of Lerna, near Argos.

P. 140   *Synod of Thermopylae*: an ancient Hellenic council, called 'Amphictyonic' after its legendary founder, Amphictyon, assembled near Thermopylae.

P. 143   *Cheiron*: a 'good' centaur, who had educated Heracles and had been accidentally wounded by him in his battle with the lawless tribe.

P. 153   *Wife of Zeus*: Hera, who persecuted Heracles from his birth and caused him to be enslaved to Eurystheus, king of Argos, at whose command he performed his famous 'labours'. Of his numerous adversaries Heracles, later in this speech, mentions six: the Nemean Lion, the Hydra of Lerna, the Centaurs, the Erymanthian Boar, Cerberus, and the Dragon of the Hesperides.

P. 157   *Selli*: priests of Zeus, members of a prehistoric tribe dwelling around Dodona.

P. 161   The death of Heracles, by the generally accepted account, did not exactly take the form foreshadowed in this play. Making his way alone up the mountain, he contrived to rear his own pyre, and it was his friend Philoctetes whom he eventually persuaded to kindle the pyre, in return for the gift of the bow and poisoned arrows. In the play *Philoctetes* the gift of the weapons is assumed, though Philoctetes is there said to have thrown Heracles into the volcano of Lemnos.

Some authorities assign the last six lines of the play to Hyllus, and others to the Chorus; and some take them to be addressed to Iole. They are in fact addressed to 'Woman' (in the singular); but this could refer to the chorus-leader, or the chorus generally, whereas it is unlikely that Iole would be on the stage at this point. We do not know that Sophocles invariably gave the chorus the last word; I therefore adopt what seems to be the most fitting conclusion.

P. 163   *Lemnos:* the island was in fact a large one and legends of the earliest times gave it inhabitants and a king. Its volcanic character is reflected in the story of Hephaestus having fallen there when thrown out of heaven. Other dramatic versions of the Philoctetes story introduced a chorus of Lemnian inhabitants; by dispensing with these, Sophocles has considerably enhanced the atmosphere of Philoctetes' lonely exile, while his chorus of Greek sailors bring a lively touch of realism to the play.

P. 176   *Ajax the Great:* to distinguish him from the 'lesser' Ajax, son of Oileus (cf. *Iliad*)

         Sisyphus: a legendary king of Corinth, whose crafty misdeeds earned him the famous 'rolling stone' punishment in Hades. The aspersion that Odysseus was the offspring of this malefactor, and no true son of Laertes, is a part of post-Homeric legend which is consonant with the deceitful character given to Odysseus for the purposes of this play.

P. 177   *Son of Tydeus:* Diomedes.

P. 185   *A ravisher bold:* Ixion, who attempted to seduce Hera, the wife of Zeus.

P. 187   *Lord of the Bronze Shield:* Heracles

Discover more about our forthcoming books through Penguin's FREE newspaper...

Penguin
Quarterly

It's packed with:

- exciting features
- author interviews
- previews & reviews
- books from your favourite films & TV series
- exclusive competitions & much, much more...

READ MORE IN PENGUIN

In every corner of the world, on every subject under the sun, Penguin represents quality and variety – the very best in publishing today.

For complete information about books available from Penguin – including Puffins, Penguin Classics and Arkana – and how to order them, write to us at the appropriate address below. Please note that for copyright reasons the selection of books varies from country to country.

In the United Kingdom: Please write to *Dept. JC, Penguin Books Ltd, FREEPOST, West Drayton, Middlesex UB7 OBR*

If you have any difficulty in obtaining a title, please send your order with the correct money, plus ten per cent for postage and packaging, to *PO Box No. 11, West Drayton, Middlesex UB7 OBR*

In the United States: Please write to *Penguin USA Inc., 375 Hudson Street, New York, NY 10014*

In Canada: Please write to *Penguin Books Canada Ltd, 10 Alcorn Avenue, Suite 300, Toronto, Ontario M4V 3B2*

In Australia: Please write to *Penguin Books Australia Ltd, 487 Maroondah Highway, Ringwood, Victoria 3134*

In New Zealand: Please write to *Penguin Books (NZ) Ltd,182–190 Wairau Road, Private Bag, Takapuna, Auckland 9*

In India: Please write to *Penguin Books India Pvt Ltd, 706 Eros Apartments, 56 Nehru Place, New Delhi 110 019*

In the Netherlands: Please write to *Penguin Books Netherlands B.V., Keizersgracht 231 NL–1016 DV Amsterdam*

In Germany: Please write to *Penguin Books Deutschland GmbH, Friedrichstrasse 10–12, W–6000 Frankfurt/Main 1*

In Spain: Please write to *Penguin Books S. A., C. San Bernardo 117–6° E–28015 Madrid*

In Italy: Please write to *Penguin Italia s.r.l., Via Felice Casati 20, I–20124 Milano*

In France: Please write to *Penguin France S. A., 17 rue Lejeune, F–31000 Toulouse*

In Japan: Please write to *Penguin Books Japan, Ishikiribashi Building, 2–5–4, Suido, Bunkyo-ku, Tokyo 112*

In Greece: Please write to *Penguin Hellas Ltd, Dimocritou 3, GR–106 71 Athens*

In South Africa: Please write to *Longman Penguin Southern Africa (Pty) Ltd, Private Bag X08, Bertsham 2013*

READ MORE IN PENGUIN

A CHOICE OF CLASSICS

Aeschylus	**The Oresteian Trilogy**
	Prometheus Bound/The Suppliants/Seven Against Thebes/The Persians
Aesop	**Fables**
Ammianus Marcellinus	**The Later Roman Empire (AD 354–378)**
Apollonius of Rhodes	**The Voyage of Argo**
Apuleius	**The Golden Ass**
Aristophanes	**The Knights/Peace/The Birds/The Assemblywomen/Wealth**
	Lysistrata/The Acharnians/The Clouds
	The Wasps/The Poet and the Women/ The Frogs
Aristotle	**The Art of Rhetoric**
	The Athenian Constitution
	Ethics
	The Politics
	De Anima
Arrian	**The Campaigns of Alexander**
St Augustine	**City of God**
	Confessions
Boethius	**The Consolation of Philosophy**
Caesar	**The Civil War**
	The Conquest of Gaul
Catullus	**Poems**
Cicero	**The Murder Trials**
	The Nature of the Gods
	On the Good Life
	Selected Letters
	Selected Political Speeches
	Selected Works
Euripides	**Alcestis/Iphigenia in Tauris/Hippolytus**
	The Bacchae/Ion/The Women of Troy/ Helen
	Medea/Hecabe/Electra/Heracles
	Orestes/The Children of Heracles/ Andromache/The Suppliant Women/ The PhoenicianWomen/Iphigenia in Aulis

READ MORE IN PENGUIN

A CHOICE OF CLASSICS

Hesiod/Theognis	**Theogony and Works and Days/ Elegies**
Hippocrates	**Hippocratic Writings**
Homer	**The Iliad**
	The Odyssey
Horace	**Complete Odes and Epodes**
Horace/Persius	**Satires and Epistles**
Juvenal	**Sixteen Satires**
Livy	**The Early History of Rome**
	Rome and Italy
	Rome and the Mediterranean
	The War with Hannibal
Lucretius	**On the Nature of the Universe**
Marcus Aurelius	**Meditations**
Martial	**Epigrams**
Ovid	**The Erotic Poems**
	Heroides
	Metamorphoses
Pausanias	**Guide to Greece** (in two volumes)
Petronius/Seneca	**The Satyricon/The Apocolocyntosis**
Pindar	**The Odes**
Plato	**Early Socratic Dialogues**
	Gorgias
	The Last Days of Socrates (Euthyphro/ The Apology/Crito/Phaedo)
	The Laws
	Phaedrus and Letters VII and VIII
	Philebus
	Protagoras and Meno
	The Republic
	The Symposium
	Theaetetus
	Timaeus and Critias

READ MORE IN PENGUIN

A CHOICE OF CLASSICS

Plautus	**The Pot of Gold/The Prisoners/The Brothers Menaechmus/The Swaggering Soldier/Pseudolus**
	The Rope/Amphitryo/The Ghost/A Three-Dollar Day
Pliny	**The Letters of the Younger Pliny**
Pliny the Elder	**Natural History**
Plotinus	**The Enneads**
Plutarch	**The Age of Alexander** (Nine Greek Lives)
	The Fall of the Roman Republic (Six Lives)
	The Makers of Rome (Nine Lives)
	The Rise and Fall of Athens (Nine Greek Lives)
	Plutarch on Sparta
Polybius	**The Rise of the Roman Empire**
Procopius	**The Secret History**
Propertius	**The Poems**
Quintus Curtius Rufus	**The History of Alexander**
Sallust	**The Jugurthine War** and **The Conspiracy of Cataline**
Seneca	**Four Tragedies** and **Octavia**
	Letters from a Stoic
Sophocles	**Electra/Women of Trachis/Philoctetes/Ajax**
	The Theban Plays
Suetonius	**The Twelve Caesars**
Tacitus	**The Agricola** and **The Germania**
	The Annals of Imperial Rome
	The Histories
Terence	**The Comedies (The Girl from Andros/The Self-Tormentor/TheEunuch/Phormio/The Mother-in-Law/The Brothers)**
Thucydides	**The History of the Peloponnesian War**
Virgil	**The Aeneid**
	The Eclogues
	The Georgics
Xenophon	**Conversations of Socrates**
	A History of My Times
	The Persian Expedition